Unfinished Business

Unfinished Business

Black Women, the Black Church,
and the Struggle to Thrive in America

KERI DAY

ORBIS BOOKS

Maryknoll, New York 10545

Founded in 1970, Orbis Books endeavors to publish works that enlighten the mind, nourish the spirit, and challenge the conscience. The publishing arm of the Maryknoll Fathers and Brothers, Orbis seeks to explore the global dimensions of the Christian faith and mission, to invite dialogue with diverse cultures and religious traditions, and to serve the cause of reconciliation and peace. The books published reflect the views of their authors and do not represent the official position of the Maryknoll Society. To learn more about Maryknoll and Orbis Books, please visit our website at www.maryknollsociety.org.

Library of Congress Cataloging-in-Publication Data

Day, Keri.
   Unfinished business : Black women, the Black church, and the struggle to thrive in America / Keri Day.
      p. cm.
   Includes bibliographical references (p.   ) and index.
   ISBN 978–1–57075–981–9 (pbk.); ISBN 978–1–60833–215–1 (ebook)
   1. African American churches. 2. Church work with women—United States. 3. Church work with the poor—United States. I. Title.
   BR563.N4D39 2012
   277.3'083082—dc23
                                                                2012012795

To my grandmother,
Rose Day,
who embodied what it means
to speak on behalf of those
who are vulnerable and disenfranchised.

Contents

Acknowledgments

I thank my mother and father, Connie Woods and Wilbur Day, as well as their respective spouses, for their unequivocal support as I live out my vocational call within theological education. My family has supported me through the highs and lows of writing this book, which began as my doctoral dissertation.

I also have the honor of thanking my doctoral and dissertation adviser at Vanderbilt University, Victor Anderson, who intellectually challenged me beyond measure. I am grateful for the many conversations we had on issues of poverty, critical social theory, and womanist/feminist studies. He taught me the value of Socratic exchange. He remains my most fierce interlocutor. I also want to acknowledge Ted Smith, Melissa Snarr, and Lewis Baldwin, dissertation committee members who helped me think through questions that find their expression in this text. I also am grateful for the intellectual community I had while completing my studies at Vanderbilt's Graduate Department of Religion. This community includes Tamura Lomax, Monique Moultrie, Christophe Ringer, Asante Todd, Brandon McCormack, Nicole Phillips, Tamara Lewis, Kimberly Russaw, and so many more. They also pushed me to think critically on issues related to poor black women.

I also thank Stacey Floyd-Thomas and Anthony Pinn for their commitment in helping me navigate the publishing industry in order to find a "home" for this text.

I am also grateful for my Brite Divinity faculty colleagues, who have discussed with me many of the ideas you find in this text. The conversations and larger intellectual work of Stephen Sprinkle, Warren Carter, and Joretta Marshall have particularly helped me think about some of the concepts I deploy. The students at Brite also "keep me on my toes," testing my ideas and arguments in the various seminars and courses I teach. I also thank two womanist colleagues and sisters in the Dallas/Fort Worth area who have helped me clarify my ideas and arguments, Melanie Harris and Evelyn Parker. Thanks so much, sisters.

Finally, I also am thankful for the invaluable support of Rev. Dr. Fredrick Douglas Haynes and Friendship West Baptist Church, particularly the ministers in training community (MIT). I have spent a lot of time in conversation and communion with this black church ministry. I am grateful that there are models within the black church that take issues of black poverty seriously. I look forward to connecting "church and academy" as I continue to articulate visions of justice and social transformation within our communities and nation.

Introduction

Black Women's Poverty Revisited

In February 2009, I sat watching *20/20* as Diane Sawyer interviewed rural poor white persons in a special program entitled, "A Hidden America: Children of the Mountains." In this documentary Sawyer describes Central Appalachia in Kentucky as a place where children and families face unthinkable conditions, including a poverty rate three times the national rate, the shortest life span in the nation, toothlessness, cancer, depression, and an epidemic of prescription-drug abuse. Sawyer hearkens back to the days of Robert Kennedy, who called on the rest of America to reach out and help the people of Appalachia. For Sawyer, these impoverished people are the "forgotten and hidden America" whose ancestors go back to the American legendary soldiers and pioneers such as Davy Crockett and Daniel Boone. She interviewed the children and parents of Appalachia and declared them heroes who fight against all odds despite their depressing socioeconomic conditions. Structural problems continue to inhibit their quality of life, producing cultural hopelessness and despair for many of them. Yet, Sawyer concluded, these children and families have a resilient spirit of hope as they continue to fight such debilitating odds in search for a better life.

I sat there completely shocked. I was very grateful that people facing intergenerational cycles of poverty were seen as victims of economic structures and institutions that perpetuate such poverty and despair. However, I couldn't help but notice that all the bodies within this report were *white*. Sawyer used structural explanations of poverty when describing the rural, impoverished white people of Appalachia, and I immediately thought of the many insidious cultural representations of black poverty in America. Sawyer's portrayal was a stark contrast to the ways in which black poverty in America has tended to be associated with personal irresponsibility. Why has black poverty been associated with personal irresponsibility to the exclusion of wider structural explanations?

The contradictions associated with American cultural representations of poverty amazed me. While the white people of Appalachia are described as a heroic and forgotten group that suffers from oppressive structures, black poverty is popularly equated with laziness and criminality. Within the

personal irresponsibility!

Media

media, black poverty is frequently framed as singularly due to the moral culpability of blacks themselves. Within American culture, media images tend to depict poor blacks not as a forgotten group but as a group that has forgotten the importance of hard work, discipline, and morality. Specifically, poor black women are severely castigated as demanding matriarchs who emasculate black men and nurture black criminals. These women are represented as morally problematic and dependent on the money of good tax-paying citizens. Because black women are often blamed for the deprivation and moral problems of society, I decided to take a closer look at the struggles of poor black women and question assumptions about poor black women's presumed personal irresponsibility.

Poor black women by far are not irresponsible. The black women now vilified by the media were a part of the rural community in which I grew up and were in no way irresponsible. They braided my hair, sang in the choir with me, and taught me how to be industrious and self-sufficient. Simply put, poor black women are often used as signifiers for poverty that is self-caused and self-generated in America. I wondered when *20/20* might do a program on poor blacks (such as black women) that focused on the structural problems that lead to intergenerational cycles of deprivation and despair for them. In what ways can poor black women be described as a "forgotten group" in America, a group that needs to be reached out to and helped due to structural factors that inhibit its members' quality of life and flourishing? Because advanced capitalism in America and its objective and subjective goods (such as food, work, cultural respect, social recognition, and so on) tend to exclude poor black women's sense of flourishing and thriving, these women stand in need of both economic relief and cultural respect.

Advanced Capitalism

✓   Neglected within American cultural life, poor blacks experience economic and social constraints as they suffer from a lack of transportation, decent housing, and a solid standard of education, the absence of healthcare, and so on. Cultural portrayals of poor blacks often depict black men as thugs or hustlers and black women as welfare queens or matriarchs. Thus I have decided to undertake a structural analysis of black women's poverty within a cultural context that identifies them as villains and the "face of poverty" in America. My focus is on poor black women because they continue to experience the most hostile and venomous cultural attacks as diverse societal institutions blame them for their poverty. But while poor black women are vilified in the media, they also experience contexts of hope and meaning by which to transcend such venomous attacks. Because their hope often comes from the Black Church and other black religious institutions, it seems reasonable that the Black Church can also serve as a context of real hope for these women who seek to escape poverty.

Vilified

transcend

structural factors

THE BLACK CHURCHES IN AMERICA

This book explores the Black Church as a black religious site that can offer not only hope and cultural flourishing for poor black women but can also participate in a project of economic justice toward their well-being. It is important to remember that the Black Church is not a monolithic entity. It is constituted by plural traditions, textures, and expressions. I therefore use the analytic category Black Church to describe the activity of black churches in America. The Black Church in the twenty-first century has become less clearly tied to its hallmark connection to social justice, reflecting increasing complexity and ambiguity. Sometimes it continues to stand within the traditions of social justice, while at other times the focus tends to be on individual prosperity and away from broader social transformation. Despite these tensions within black church spaces, poor black women can and do experience possibilities of transcendence and meaning.

Black churches have been important historical contexts wherein black people could experience economic relief and cultural flourishing. They have a long history of providing hope and cultural freedom for poor members within their own communities. Moreover, black churches continue to be sites of hope and cultural flourishing in response to the despair that threatens to grip the lives of poor black women. Cultural anthropologist Marla Frederick presents an ethnographic study of poor rural black women of Halifax County, North Carolina, and how they experience hope. In *Between Sundays: Black Women and Everyday Struggles of Faith*, she offers an anthropological analysis of their impoverished conditions and how their spirituality is both a catalyst for social interactions and an interpretive lens used in formulating responses to their harsh political and economic conditions. For Frederick, many of these women's feelings of spirituality and hope were found within the context of black churches. Although Frederick's anthropological work supports my assertion that black churches have been and continue to be sites that can provide a space wherein poor black women's individual needs and desires for communion, love, and solidarity are met, she also notes that there are black women who remain suspicious of black churches, choosing to find meaning and hope within other communal organizations.

It is crucial to recognize that the complexity and ambiguity within the history and contemporary activities of black churches are profoundly important. Christian scholars of black religion tend to gather around narrow conceptions of black religious identity, articulating nostalgic understandings of the form and function of black religious life in America. Scholars tend to see themselves as the arbiters of what is the "true black church," pessimistically evaluating black ministers of the gospel by this mythic standard of religious and racial authenticity. Consequently, our anger and disappointment surface when our projected understanding of black religion "fails to produce the Martin Luther Kings and Fannie Lou Hamers."[1] This book tries to avoid nostalgic interpretations of the Black Church in order to understand more deeply the possibilities *and* contradictions of these black religious institutions. Only by understanding the complexity and tensions of black churches can we theorize how these institutions can effectively address deprivation among their most vulnerable members.

Black religious and theological discourses have done well in relating black religious institutions such as black churches to the many socioeconomic and political problems that black communities face. In particular, black liberation theology and womanist theology have described how black churches should respond to these problems. Some womanist theologians and ethicists such as Delores S. Williams and Kelly Brown Douglas have focused on poor black women and ways in which black churches and the broader society can foster liberation, survival, and increased quality of life for them. For these womanists, black churches must reflect critically on how they can be contexts of hope and freedom for poor black women, who are often oppressed within these very institutions.

Other womanist thinkers disclose ways in which socioeconomic structures, attitudes, and public policies perpetuate intergenerational cycles of deprivation and poverty for black women. For instance, womanist theologians and ethicists such as Cheryl Townsend Gilkes and Emilie Townes explore how cultural representations affect public policy, often impeding poor black women from thriving and flourishing. These womanist thinkers also discuss how black churches can be productive contexts out of which poor black women can find meaning and hope. While I draw upon womanist theology and ethics when turning to how black churches can be contexts of hope for poor black women, this work moves beyond such discourses by offering a critique of the American political economy and by developing a concept of thriving that offers practical guidance toward economic justice for these women.

While capitalist institutions and systems perpetuate impoverishment for so many black women and their children, poverty deeply affects their human personality. Many poor black women struggle with a sense that the American system, which purports to offer respect and parity to them, is failing to do so. Due to continual systemic repression, many within poor black communities suffer from a lack of the cultural capital (respect, confidence, parity) required to self-actualize and thrive. Such hopelessness within poor black communities is often left unaddressed as poor blacks are blamed for their own poverty. We must take seriously this hopelessness, and disempowerment in general, in order to craft visions of justice that offer them hope.

cultural
capital   continual   systemic   repression,

While black religious and theological discourses tend to focus on hope when discussing the relationship of black churches to poor black women, these discourses do not develop a concept of thriving. Although black women need hope, they also need to thrive. *Thriving* refers to poor people developing the economic and cultural resources needed to participate on a par with their nonpoor peers. Economic well-being depends upon both cultural forms of respect and the restructuring of our political economy so that thriving is possible. This book advances the claim that black churches can participate in a project of thriving with and for poor black women so that economic justice can become a real possibility. However, this project of economic justice and thriving must orient itself in reference to the exploitative nature of advanced capitalism as well as the unique experiences of poor black women in the twenty-first century.

THE PROBLEM OF ADVANCED CAPITALISM

This text examines the ways in which economic inequities and cultural inequalities collude to structure adversely the economic opportunities of poor black women. I use an ideology critique, which can be described as a critique set on redeeming. As redemptive criticism, ideology critique acts as a catalyst for social change by redeeming those contradictory social ideals within capitalist structures that may be oppressive but have emancipatory potential. This form of critique examines or deconstructs class oppressions and interests but also constructs possibilities for hope and flourishing within capitalist arrangements. This particular notion of ideology critique as redeeming critique was initially articulated by critical social theorist Walter Benjamin.

Benjamin's concept of ideology critique illuminates how advanced capitalism intensifies and exacerbates class struggles. Benjamin argues that there are historical, social, and cultural influences that interact with and shape modes of production, which identifies culture and economy as separate yet interrelated spheres that determine the opportunities of oppressed communities within society.[2] Economy has its own economic ordering, which overlaps with and affects the cultural ordering within capitalist societies. Dissimilar to Marx's view of culture, Benjamin does not interpret symbolic or cultural processes as epiphenomena of economy, no more than expressions of the material base.[3] For Benjamin, and most early critical theorists, class struggles cannot be reduced to oppressive cultural forms that perpetuate class oppressions. Instead, Benjamin understands culture as discrete, affecting and interacting with modes of production. The imperatives of capitalism are reinforced "both in the conscious attempts of its apologists, literary and aesthetic heroes, and statesmen to generate a dominant culture that expresses the triumphs of capitalist modernity."[4] This dominant culture includes advertising, fashion, the endless flow of commodities, consumer fads, commercial ventures, popular literature, journalism, and more.[5] Such cultural hegemony collaborates with economic oppression, producing loss of meaning and hopelessness for marginalized persons.

Transforming an economy does not necessarily lead to change in the cultural areas of that society and vice versa. There is a need to transform both the culture and the economy in order to foster hope and thriving for the oppressed within society. Culture and economy as discrete yet inter-related influences are significant to understanding class oppression among alienated communities and to identify under what conditions hope and thriving are possible.

Additionally, Benjamin's concept of ideology critique doesn't see social critique of capitalist productions merely as "criticism oriented towards the radical destruction of capitalism" but sees it as a "redeeming" act that attempts to offer ways to promote cultural and social renewal within the contexts of capitalist processes. Benjamin moves beyond capitalism as virtue or vice. Instead, he believes that capitalist societies must undergo radical critique as a necessary prerequisite for cultural and social renewal. For him, this radical critique prepares the ground not only for a reconstruction of history (which includes the repressed perspectives of the oppressed and not merely the victors) but also for cultural renewal within society, which includes cultural, political, and theological renewal.

The Relationship between Culture and Economy

Exploring culture and economy as interrelated spheres is important because economic relief and cultural flourishing are both essential for poor black women to move out of poverty. I broadly understand *culture* to mean more than the shared norms and values within a society. Culture is not monolithic. Rather, it can be seen as a complex of layered social structures that reflect problems of domination. Cultural norms, attitudes, and practices generally function as ideological tools of the well-off, and such cultural norms and habits are seen as natural and normal instead of socially constructed from privilege and interest. Consequently, culture becomes the ground for domination—and the ground for resistance as well. While the idea of culture is more expansive than cultural representations, this book employs *culture* to discuss how cultural representations of poor black women are normalized and used as ideological tools of the wealthy and powerful.

The language of political economy describes those political ideas, structures, and norms that shape, guide, and determine economic practices and outcomes. When deploying the language of political economy, we must recognize that economic attitudes and practices in American life are always regulated by larger political values, projects, and goals. This book pushes beyond a discussion of economics merely as a science of market exchanges by disclosing how economic practices and outcomes are largely determined by social and political forces at a given historical period. America's political economy possesses certain political and economic forces that have cultivated and maintained unjust economic outcomes for poor blacks, and particularly for poor black women. The American economy and its systems of exchange are not morally neutral.

In fact, America's political economy is deeply influenced by advanced capitalist ideologies and practices. As used here, *advanced capitalism* describes how capitalism in the second half of the twentieth century colonized every aspect of life, turning everything into a commodity or transaction.[6] Over time, advanced capitalism and its systems of commodification have become cultural and political values that inform social relations. For example, within advanced capitalism labor is no longer seen as a human capability worthy of respect but rather as a commodity that is exchanged to maximize profit. Labor has lost its humanizing element and become depersonalized, nothing more than another commodity that is a part of economic transactions. Advanced capitalism sponsors a type of morality that dehumanizes social relations so that they are used instrumentally as a means toward the ends of market goals. Simply put, an advanced capitalist political economy promotes commodity fetishism in which social relationships among people are expressed as relationships among things (commodities and money).[7]

The Role of Neo-liberal Values

Advanced capitalist practices also employ neo-liberal values to shape and determine economic outcomes. Neo-liberalism carries a belief in the "invisible hand" of a free market to regulate transactions among individuals; thus state regulation of or government intervention in the economy are deemed both unnatural and adverse. Neo-liberalism privileges an economic structure that resists government oversight and intervention and also adheres to a philosophy of success through individual action and merit. Individuals are responsible for their economic success or failure, not the market or institutional structures. Individual merit and ambition are the hallmarks of responsible and deserving citizens, which in turn suggests that poor persons are irresponsible, undeserving, and lacking in ambition and merit.[8]

Such neo-liberal attitudes can be seen in the myth of meritocracy, which determines an individual's success or failure based upon his or her merit in relation to work, savings, investment, and risk. This myth does not consider any institutional or structural constraints that impede individual flourishing. Advanced capitalism generally benefits elite communities and dismisses ways in which its structural constraints perpetuate poverty among disadvantaged communities.

America's advanced capitalism is imbued with neo-liberal political meanings, commitments, and ideas that engender oppressive outcomes for poor persons within America, especially for black women, the focus of this book. It is the selfish political interests of the wealthy that usually guide economic practices within the United States, and the rich get richer and the poor grow poorer.

Poor black women and their children are often the most vulnerable. A vision of economic justice is desperately needed within our country, a vision that challenges America's capitalist economy and privileges economic parity *for all*. The debate on poverty must take a new course. Poor blacks, particularly poor black women, must not be construed as the "face" of American poverty. Instead, capitalist systems and practices must be exposed and deconstructed in order to challenge the economic inequities and constraints that exacerbate cycles of deprivation for the poor.

THE NEW WAYS BLACK POVERTY ARTICULATES ITSELF

Describing deprived black women as "poor black women" has its limitations. Do black women who experience deprivation consider themselves poor? Clearly, referring to economically challenged black women as poor presents certain limitations and social dangers because many of these women may not choose to name or identify themselves as poor. With this in mind, I use the term *the poor* as an *economic marker* that says something about inequitable structures that contribute toward many black women possessing insufficient income and lacking the economic and cultural assets needed to develop their human capacity to thrive and flourish.

I maintain that poverty is not merely an insufficiency of income. Impoverishment is also created and exacerbated by a lack of the assets needed permanently to leave what are often intergenerational cycles of deprivation. Poverty is often denoted as being below a certain level of income. For example, according to the Department of Health and Human Resources, the 2011 poverty-level line for a family of four was set at $22,350 a year; those below this line were assumed to be unable to meet their basic material needs. However, *poverty* as used here designates much more than poverty-level lines. Poverty is produced and reproduced when the poor are locked out of America's wealth-producing structures. Consequently, poor black women, as discussed here, are those who are *both income and asset deficient*. If black religious institutions, including black churches, are going to respond effectively to poor black women, they must expand their understandings of poverty, moving beyond an income-focused perspective.

GROWTH OF AN AMERICAN UNDERCLASS

Black churches must also see black women's poverty as situated within an American underclass. This underclass includes poor persons across racial groups. Class standing here refers to a Marxist notion of class in which class fundamentally expresses relationships among modes of production. In order to have class standing, a person must be either a capitalist producer or a laborer. However, America's underclass endures conditions today that do not make class standing possible, such as lack of adequate education, unemployment and underemployment, high rates of incarceration, and homelessness. These factors identify an American underclass that commonly experiences chronic, persisting experiences of economic and cultural invisibility and powerlessness.

Poor black women are a part of an American underclass that is not ethnic specific; the underclass includes poor whites, poor Latinos/as, poor Native Americans, and other impoverished racial groups. This challenges the usual assumptions that identify race as the primary determinate of black women's poverty. Intergenerational cycles of deprivation among black women should not be understood as due solely to racial oppression and/or gender discrimination. To date, black religious and theological discourses have primarily articulated black women's poverty in terms of both racial and gender injustice without substantively exploring the increasing significance or nature of class injustice. Class does matter.

The impoverishment of black women has been exacerbated by shifts in the American political economy over the last four decades. Even if racism definitively ended in the United States, poor black women would not be able to lift themselves out of poverty without some basic restructuring of America's wealth-producing institutions. These economic shifts in America's economy, described at length in Chapter 3, have contributed to a growing American underclass that includes blacks, whites, Hispanics, and some other ethnic groups. Although poor black women experience poverty in qualitatively different ways due to racial injustice, their experiences of poverty cannot be attributed singularly or primarily to racial and gender oppression.

This observation is important. The increasing significance of class challenges the assumption that racial justice will lead to the amelioration of black poverty. The amelioration of black poverty requires racial and gender justice along with economic justice. Any project of thriving with and for poor black women must fashion a vision of economic justice that addresses the economic inequities and inequalities experienced by the American underclass. Because black churches have a history of class-based movements for economic justice, they may be able to revive such class-based movements to bring about thriving for the poor, especially for poor black women.

THE GOAL AND STRUCTURE OF THIS BOOK

A specific aim of this book is to develop a concept of thriving. I maintain that black religious institutions, including black churches, can effectively participate in a project of thriving with and for poor black women. Black churches can help form the vanguard in charting a program of thriving that will bring hope and meaning to the daily lives of impoverished black women. I believe that black churches must (1) critically revisit their anti-poverty strategies for the poor, including any faith-based initiatives; (2) revive a multi-ethnic, class-based movement for economic justice that draws upon the ideals of the Poor People's Campaign; (3) examine and critique unhealthy prosperity gospel theologies that blame the poor by providing more holistic visions of prosperity and well-being; and (4) promote public policies that focus on asset building for the poor across racial communities.

My overall goal is to evaluate the social implications of black women's poverty in this country and offer an understanding of thriving that can address their suffering and alienation. My approach is interdisciplinary, drawing on the work of black sociologists and cultural theorists on black poverty, on philosophical and theological insights about liberation and thriving, and critical historical questions on how interlocking oppressions such as race, class, gender, and sexuality have affected and continue to affect black women's experiences of deprivation. This interdisciplinary approach will aid in understanding the realities of poverty black women endure and what political and religious responses would be most appropriate. Other scholars I have turned to include black sociologists such as Patricia Hill Collins and Marcellus Andrews, black cultural anthropologists such as Marla Frederick and Dána-Ain Davis, and black historians such as Barbara Savage, among others.

My intent throughout is not to supplant the current discussion of poverty within the black community but to expand it. I seek to tell a new story about black women's poverty over the past four decades and to demonstrate the possibilities of changing impoverishment into hope and flourishing. While black churches attempt to be contexts of transcendence wherein poor black women can find hope and meaning, these churches often do not possess a sophisticated understanding of economic institutions and their exploitative practices. This inhibits what they are able to accomplish in the long term.

Chapter 1 argues that understanding black churches as *complex* sites of meaning-making and communities of transcendence for poor black women can enable them to participate effectively in projects of hope and thriving. In *The Social Teachings of the Black Church*, Peter Paris describes the early Black Church as a "surrogate world" for black communities.

However, womanist theological scholars such as Delores Williams have critiqued this image of a surrogate world, arguing that instead many black women encounter church spaces as "wilderness experiences." Both images are partially true; however, they often overly influence discussions on the significance and importance of black churches. When employed in a reductive way, they exclude other images that more adequately explore the range of black women's experiences within black church contexts. Drawing on Marla Frederick, I maintain that many poor black women experience the Black Church as a community of transcendence, helping them to hope and to find meaning.

Chapter 2 explores a particular anti-poverty strategy that black churches use in relation to poor black women, that of faith-based initiatives. Some black churches employ charitable-choice approaches or faith-based initiatives as part of their strategies to empower poor women to transcend their poverty. While this approach to poverty seeks to empower these women to find hope and meaning, it usually fails to address the larger structural injustices that perpetuate and exacerbate such poverty. Yes, poor black women need to have the basic resources necessary for survival and thriving. However, they also need, as do black church leaders, to learn how to grapple with and challenge the larger questions of structural injustice and destructive values and ideologies that sustain such injustice. Black churches must grasp the significance of the many economic and social forces that determine public policy.

Chapters 3 and 4 turn to the economic inequities and policy miseries poor black women endure as a part of an American underclass. Chapter 3 contends that black churches would do well to cultivate political wisdom about the contemporary problem of black women in order to counteract many churches' usual and often misleading assumptions. Political wisdom involves first of all acknowledging the new forms of economic inequities that poor black women experience that prevent them from entering a "level playing field" with middle- and upper-class persons, including members of those groups who are African America.

Political wisdom also involves acknowledging that there are multiple black Americas. Poor black women's oppressive experiences are qualitatively different from those of women in middle- and upper-class black communities. Consequently, race cannot be seen as the sole determinant of these women's opportunities. Instead, poor black women's experiences of poverty can be grasped and understood more adequately by exploring historical shifts in the American political economy and how these shifts intensify and worsen their experiences of deprivation. The work of black sociologist Patricia Hill Collins provides a comprehensive portrait of the socioeconomic experiences of poor black women. Again, class matters.

Chapter 4 contends that current welfare reform policies reinforce the regulation and control of poor black women's lives. Religious communities in particular, including black churches, must acknowledge and challenge how racist and conservative values have shaped welfare policy in America. Public policy is not unrelated to religious values in American life. Instead, policy feeds upon and draws its legitimacy from the Protestant religious values that many black churches embrace; the result is often to demonize poor black women. This chapter analyzes the ways in which religious values adversely affect welfare reform. Drawing on the work of Dána-Ain Davis, it also explores how welfare collaborates with the "new Jane Crow," a legalized racist system that is creating a new caste structure among women of color. As it is increasingly shaped by this new Jane Crow, welfare policy has become a form of structural violence that continues negatively to control and regulate the lives of poor black women.

The final three chapters explore the conditions under which thriving would be possible for poor black women, including how black churches might morally respond to the economic and policy constraints poor black women endure. Because poor black women are part of a larger American underclass that goes across racial affiliations, class-based responses are extremely important. Chapter 5 explores the Poor People's Campaign, a class-based movement in the 1960s that sought to ameliorate poverty, suggesting that such a campaign should be revived as a class-based, multi-ethnic movement for economic justice.

Chapter 6 argues that in order for a Poor People's Campaign movement to be revived within black churches, many black churches must critique their current prosperity gospel theologies and fashion a more complex understanding of prosperity. Many current teachings of a prosperity gospel do not consider how free-market, individualistic notions of prosperity undermine communal well-being and flourishing. Black churches can advance a new kind of prosperity gospel that fosters the ideals of social trust, compassion, inclusion, and participation among all poor persons, and especially among poor black women.

Finally, Chapter 7 explores how a class-based concept of thriving can help support a revival of a multi-ethnic, class-based movement for economic justice; it maintains that a class-based concept of thriving must advance an asset-building approach within public policy. A morally adequate response to poverty must be based on a multi-ethnic, class-based concept of thriving that goes beyond traditional income-based strategies. To be certain, this asset-building approach articulates a long-term moral vision about ways to ameliorate poverty by developing the capabilities of the poor to participate on a par with their peers as contributing members within society.

In sum, my goal is to revisit why class matters and why black women's opportunity to thrive is really about the thriving of *all* poor persons. Most important, I attempt to articulate why black churches matter to the thriving of poor people and to the strengthening of America's democratic project as a land of liberty, equality, and opportunity for all.

1

Is the Black Church "Home" for Poor Black Women?

"Woman, thou art loosed!" T. D. Jakes exclaims as women around the stadium rise to their feet, clapping their hands, and chanting their own sense of possibilities and deliverance from financial battles, relationship hurts, and professional setbacks. Upon entering one of Jakes's women's conferences, you can feel a groundswell of excitement and hope as women "high-five" one another, dancing in the crowded aisles and jumping up and down to the organ crooning in the background.

Although thousands of women flock to stadiums to hear Jakes preach, his critics also abound. In fact, Jakes's critics often interpret him as a black capitalist who uses theatrical multimedia strategies to exploit black women, especially those who are working class or poor. While I do not seek to discount or vindicate Jakes's personal intentions or ministry, the underlying concern of these criticisms is intriguing. In part, critics are concerned that the Black Church is less than a safe haven or "home" for black women, particularly poor black women, who are exploited in our wider, profit-driven, capitalist culture. This is a legitimate concern. Are black churches "homes" or "safe havens" for poor black women, or are they becoming religious institutions driven by the larger demands of our capitalist society?

The well-being of many poor black women is intimately related to black churches. First, black women, historically and now, constitute the majority of black church members and are presently the most devoted supporters of such churches (as is generally true of American Protestant churches).[1] A large percentage of economically disadvantaged black women are quite active in black churches. They lead within the pastorate, sing in choirs, bake food for congregational dinners, participate in organizing financial matters, and more. As a result, black churches are important when discussing poor black women's sense of flourishing and well-being. Second, some black liberation and womanist theologies call on black churches to be the primary vehicles for empowering black communities. However, this call for the black churches to be the primary site of social transformation is to rely on an institution that was and remains largely male led but female dominated, not only in membership but also in fundraising and organizing activities.[2]

Black churches can become sites that participate in a project of hope and thriving for poor black women, but how? In order to explore this primary question, a more nuanced discussion of the Black Church is warranted. How should the Black Church be interpreted? Black theological and religious discourses have often framed the Black Church as a "surrogate world" (Peter Paris) or a "wilderness experience" (Delores S. Williams) as well as "prophetic" or "accommodationist." However, black churches should be interpreted across a broader range of understandings. The Black Church can be understood more fully as a community of transcendence in which many poor black women are able to make meaning and find hope within their complex struggles and day-to-day hardships. Describing the Black Church as a community of transcendence avoids the reductivisms of the metaphors of surrogate world and wilderness; it also captures the complexity and diversity of black churches and avoids dualistic language that would seek to pigeonhole these churches into prophetic or priestly, radical or accommodationist.

The Black Church is a community and institution that possesses multiple traditions, textures, and expressions. These multiple meanings often reveal the tensions and contradictions within the Black Church. Consequently, the Black Church needs a broader description that encompasses its diverse meanings. Drawing upon Victor Anderson and Marla Frederick, I describe the Black Church as a community of transcendence. First, it is necessary to explore the historical debates that surround the identity of the Black Church. Second, I review two primary images that can be retrieved from black theological and religious discourses on the Black Church: the Black Church as a surrogate world, and the Black Church as a wilderness. While these two images are helpful, they remain inadequate in situating the Black Church within its widest possible range of understandings.

THE BLACK CHURCH AS AN INSTITUTION

There has been an ongoing conversation between the humanities and the social sciences on the Black Church. On the one hand, for some black theological scholars, the Black Church has largely been characterized by its priestly and prophetic descriptions. These two descriptions are seen as constituting a "black church tradition." On the other hand, black religious and sociological scholars have described the Black Church as an institution, a human community of persons that possesses a religious worldview and orientation that structure its relational ties, filial bonds, and sets of practices. While the first set of scholars interprets the Black

Church as theological, the second set interprets the Black Church as primarily sociological.[3]

Because black churches constitute a diversity of religious traditions, I am aware that using *the Black Church* has linguistic limitations. However, I use the term as a category with both theological and sociological meaning. Religious ethicist James Gustafson's description of the church as a "human and natural community" is helpful when describing the Black Church as both theologically and sociologically constructed. For Gustafson, the church is a human and natural community (an institution) in that its internal socialization governs the self-identity of its community in the same way as other human communities (professional organizations, economic organizations, and so on). Gustafson argues that the church is not distinctive from other human communities by its identification as a transcendent "holy community" that claims moral exceptionalism; rather, the church is distinctive in the sense that it says something of religious significance about itself in relation to the world.[4] The church is distinctive and different in that it makes theological claims about itself in relation to God, Jesus, and the broader society.

Gustafson argues that relying on "traditional doctrinal terms inherently oversimplifies and distorts the Church."[5] While traditional doctrinal language used to describe the church aids one in understanding the church as a confessional community, it does not help one understand the church as an institution that finds its range of meanings in its social processes, institutional rituals, and sets of practices. However, "social science and philosophy [do] not satisfactorily interpret life in the Church" because "social processes do not fully explain the meaning of Christian life in the Church." Consequently, Gustafson concludes that a "sociological oversimplification is as inadequate as a theological one."[6] Both are needed in order to understand the church as a confessional community and a social institution.

My interpretation of the Black Church as both a theological and sociological construct—confessional community and human institution—questions a particular meta-narrative in relationship to it. I question the theological position that reduces the Black Church to its prophetic witness. Are black churches to be primarily understood as prophetic? Have black churches historically expressed their moral agency in connection with radical politics toward social transformation? The Black Church has always experienced tensions and contradictions over its prophetic identity and witness, which belies interpreting it as essentially prophetic and radical.

The assumption that the Black Church has been essentially liberationist in character—a social change agent within the history and memory of black communities—either dismisses or ignores the actual historical and contemporary disagreements that continue to exist about its prophetic identity.

While there is a great measure of truth in the assumption of its liberative character at particular moments within American history, the assumption that the Black Church is to be equated with a prophetic tradition often overly influences discussions of the Black Church, resulting in failure to situate the Black Church within a broader range of historical understandings. Most important, as a religious ethicist deeply invested in the life of black churches I am concerned that this assumption does not allow for an intellectually honest reading of the history of black churches in America. It is essential to explore the real *complexities and ambiguities* associated with the history of black churches in order to understand how they might strengthen themselves as sites and contexts of hope and transcendence for all their members, including poor black women.

THE BLACK CHURCH: A PROPHETIC TRADITION?

In the last few decades a growing body of literature suggests the Black Church can and/or should be primarily interpreted as prophetic within black communal life and the wider society. This refers to a tradition that focuses on radically denouncing and critiquing structural oppression and social injustices such as racism, sexism, classism, heterosexism and other forms of inequality. However, the history of black churches demonstrates that debate has always existed over whether black churches were "living into" their prophetic declarations. Barbara Savage's work in this area is compelling. As a historian, she questions whether a black church tradition should ever be interpreted, historically or contemporarily, as prophetic and radical. Savage examines the history of debates on the role of black religion, and particularly black churches, in relation to structural transformation. Retrieving a history of debates before, during, and after the Civil Rights movement, Savage provides evidence of many ambiguities, tensions, and complexities when describing the Black Church as politically revolutionary and radically prophetic.

A Historical Look at the Black Church

During post-Emancipation and into the nascent years of radical Reconstruction (1863–77), black communities established their own religious institutions, primarily in the form of Baptist churches throughout the South. Because literacy was not yet widespread, "many of the emerging black political leaders were ministers. Empowered by their literacy, they played a prominent role in building black churches, which then served as the first forums for collective political organizing."[7] Black churches not only served as educational, social, and political institutions for blacks but were also linked to the memory of the black community's enslaved ancestors. During slavery, hope among black communities contributed to the continuing struggle to realize the possibilities of American democracy. Black churches were understood as sites that participated in this hope for political, social, and spiritual freedom and self-determination.

Yet, as the policies of Reconstruction transitioned from the "formulation phase" to implementation, public discussions about black religion were "marked by a profound unease with the legacy of spiritual practices of enslaved people, which caused many elite and educated blacks to question if the Black Church could ultimately remedy the structural evils within the larger society."[8] Many blacks viewed the cultural heritage of the enslaved as antiquated and primitive, tainted by the sins of slavery and marked by pagan retentions from Africa,[9] and many within black communities thought that black Christianity as a "slave religion" had run its course. Many argued that black Christianity had lost its political potency to meet the new demands of a more modern struggle against racial oppression.[10] The role of black churches in the political project of black liberation was thrown into question, causing deep anxiety about how black churches would participate in the project of Reconstruction and the larger project of American democracy.

Throughout most of the nineteenth and early twentieth centuries, quite different black scholars settled on a consensus that the "Negro church" was a failed institution that had plunged into political irrelevancy by the end of the Reconstruction period. Prominent academically trained black intellectuals and popular culture leaders such as W. E. B. Du Bois, Fannie Williams, Carter G. Woodson, and Nannie Boroughs wrote about black religion and black churches as first and foremost an innate "problem" for the race. For instance, although early in his career Woodson described the Black Church as an "All Comprehending Institution" that helped blacks creatively survive through educational training and cultural building, he also concluded that black churches were divisive rather than unifying due to an intense rivalry in the leadership and the squandering of resources.[11] He often described the Black Church as an institution used primarily for the benefit of the "gatekeepers," being individuals who were in charge.

Like Woodson, Fannie Williams berated the Black Church as politically impotent. She attributed her disappointment with black churches to the male ministerial domination of church leadership. She described black preachers as "corrupt" and "ignorant."[12] These black leaders and thinkers challenged the widely accepted notion that black churches were understood primarily as liberative agents within their communities and the larger society.

Social scientists also lamented the negative psychological influences of black churches on youth and on the prospects of political activism. St. Clair

Drake's and Horace Cayton's *Black Metropolis* as well as Gunnar Myrdal's *American Dilemma* introduced ordinary black people as subjects who were able to articulate their own ideas about the possibilities and limitations of their churches. While ordinary church members saw the Black Church as a place of refuge, they remained dubious about the Black Church's political leadership within the wider society. The people interviewed "distinguish their resentment of failed ministerial leadership from their embrace of the nurturance and spiritual respite that churches offer; they applaud the churches' role in social and community service, but urge that more financial resources be directed to that effort and away from the clergy's personal enrichment and self-aggrandizement."[13] Such studies demonstrate that the idea of the Black church today as a liberative change agent is perhaps more widely accepted by some educated elites than by the masses of black church members.

Even in the latter part of the twentieth century black churches were still conflicted on the relationship between religion and politics. While a cadre of black churches were at the forefront of racial equality during the Civil Rights movement, this movement does not reflect "a black church tradition" in which black churches en masse participated. To be certain, the Civil Rights movement was primarily a black religious movement that challenged racist, white, imperial structures. However, a wide array of black churches and even black denominations did not support the "unlawful" methods and strategies of the Civil Rights movement, particularly during its nascent years. For example, the Church of God in Christ (COGIC) discouraged its members from participating in the political aims associated with the movement. This is significant in that COGIC was and continues to be one of the largest and fastest growing African American Pentecostal denominations in the United States. Other local black churches across the nation also dissuaded their parishioners from directly participating in the movement.

Black denominations and churches such as COGIC discouraged participation because of their theological understandings. COGIC's members' understanding of salvation and redemption was rooted in a strong eschatology that articulated the imminent return of Jesus. In the 1960s COGIC interpreted justice issues as issues that would ultimately be resolved by God in the coming eschaton.[14] Because of these core theological convictions, it remained separate from civil rights demonstrations and protests (although black denominations such as COGIC eventually supported the Civil Rights movement with the passing of the Civil Rights Act in 1964). While COGIC has evolved in its theological understandings in the last decade to include liberation and structural justice as essential to its Christian duty, these sentiments of religious and political separatism were embraced for much of its life. Most black churches (primarily Baptist) that participated in the movement were part of a *minority* among black churches participating at the height of the Civil Rights movement.

Such evidence calls into question the notion that the black church tradition has historically been understood as prophetic, as a social change agent within larger oppressive institutions. Instead, these studies show that the masses of black people, as well as the educated elite, still saw the future of black communities as dependent on *reforming* the one entity controlled by black people. The black scholars who challenged the prevailing popular conceptions of black churches constructed a remarkable critique of the limitations and shortcomings of African American religious institutions and called for a reformation of the "Negro church."

Black scholars not only discussed how to reform black churches in order to make them more politically potent and prophetic within society. They also differed on whether black churches should be seen as *central* sites of liberation and flourishing for black communities. For example, Nannie Boroughs had very clear views on how black communities could improve their political and economic position. She saw black economic institutions as central to black liberation and called on black Americans to invest their earnings in black-owned enterprises (such as black banks) that could then provide essential services to black communities. She also argued that securing the ballot was as essential as the collective use of black dollars.[15]

W. E. B. Du Bois agreed with Boroughs that black churches had tremendous economic potential as a cooperative enterprise. He noted the valuable property holdings of black churches, which were built with the pennies of the poor. They both saw the church as one site of socioeconomic and political liberation for black communities that could work collaboratively with more central political and economic institutions within black communities, such as black banks, black unions, and so on.

These historical tensions and complexities associated with black churches as social change agents debunk a particular totalizing logic. The basic categories used to describe black churches—such as prophetic or priestly, progressive or conservative, radical or accommodationist—lose their ideological power in the presence of these debates on the historical relevancy of black ecclesial institutions. When retrieving this history, the Black Church can be seen less as a prophetic tradition and more as a complex institution.

Contemporary Complexities in the Black Church

Black churches continue to embody these tensions and complexities as black religious institutions in America. Religious ethicist Jonathan Walton articulates this complexity among contemporary black churches when he refers to black televangelism, referring in particular to the ministry of T. D. Jakes. Jakes is often reduced to a messenger of the "prosperity gospel" and even described as a spiritual pimp and exploiter of women's pain. However, Walton challenges this reductive reading. He notes that Jakes's affirmation of black women as "God's Leading Ladies" counters the dominant cultural images that insult black female identity at every turn.[16]

Walton asserts:

> Whether in the forms of movies like *Big Momma's House* and *Norbit* or hypersexualized music videos, such images in contemporary popular culture extend a legacy of social constructions dating back to slavery that portray black women as socially deviant, devoid of feminine virtue, and oversexed. Black women are forced to live in a media-dominated culture where talking heads like Rush Limbaugh and Don Imus feel they can call an African American Congresswoman a "crack whore" and successful African American female student athletes "nappy-headed hos." But, through participating in their ritual of televangelism, African American women are no longer "Mammies," "Jezebels," "welfare queens," or video whores. Bishop Jakes affirms their sense of self by referring to them as worthy and deserving of love and compassion.[17]

Jakes's ministry not only gives many black women "a vision and language for thinking and acting differently in their material world" but also provides these women with ways to resist the social degradation that often accompanies their daily lives.[18] While Walton recognizes the sense of empowerment and affirmation many black women receive from the televangelism of Jakes, he also notes how Jakes's ministry suffers from a type of social accommodation that embraces the cultural myth systems that resonate with the larger culture. For example, Jakes often employs the myth of American success. His rhetoric of self-choice and moving toward economic empowerment operates with the assumption that success is based singularly on one's own merit and actions to better oneself. Such rhetoric does not attend to the structural inequities that impede black women from flourishing and thriving. The ministry of Jakes is one example of how black churches are riddled with tensions and complexities that question the traditional categories used to describe the black church.

These contradictions and tensions associated with the efficacy and relevancy of black churches prompt one to search for a more appropriate language when relating black churches to modern social ills within black communities. The language of liberation versus assimilation, or radical politics versus accommodationist politics, continues to hinder understanding black churches as complex sites for many black groups and individuals. Such categories do not capture the ambiguities of black churches as complex sites (as a confessional community and human institution) and may actually hinder a focus on the importance of flourishing and well-being for all people.

SURROGATE WORLD OR WILDERNESS?

In characterizing the Black Church I also question whether the Black Church as a surrogate world is the best metaphor to describe the relationship between black churches and poor black women today. In the 1980s, African American theological ethicist Peter Paris wrote *The Social Teaching of the Black Church*, a book that grappled with the complexities of the black church tradition. Paris argues that the "normative tradition for blacks is that tradition governed by the principle of non-racism which we call the black Christian tradition."[19] Paris examines the social conditions that gave rise to black churches in North America. Because the diabolic institutions and practices of slavery were legitimized and sanctioned by white Christianity, black people formed separate ecclesial organizations that challenged the racial ideology of white churches. Black churches were grounded in what Paris calls the "anthropological principle," a strong belief that "affirms the equality of all persons under God regardless of race or any other natural quality."[20] Black churches exposed the contradictions between biblical understandings of humanity and the practices of white churches. Because black churches provided a way for black persons to reclaim their human dignity, identity, and worth in light of the Divine, Paris names the early Black Church the "surrogate world" for the black community.

This surrogate world allowed black persons to find spiritual, socioeconomic, and political refuge and respite. In the dominant white world, slaves were degraded, debased, and rendered subhuman. In the Black Church, slaves were able to enter an alternative or substitute world that affirmed them as human beings with a culture who deserved educational opportunity, socioeconomic equality, and political power. The Black Church was a "world within a world" that challenged the internalized socialization of a white racist society. The Black Church represented a surrogate world for enslaved and oppressed blacks in which "they could exercise their communal power and create alternative narratives of black dignity and goodness."[21] This surrogate world also empowered blacks to exercise political power and educational authority in their ecclesial activities and communal practices. For Paris, the Black Church as surrogate world provided an alternative context for black people.

For Paris, the black church movement, from slavery to present, aims to institutionalize the Christian faith in a nonracist form in order to provide a context in which black communities can flourish and to critique the hypocrisy of American democracy. He interprets the formative era of the Black Church as essentially a refuge for black people that would provide a "home" where oppressed black people could self-actualize. In the end, Paris concludes that the black Christian tradition has been a lifeline and a basic principle of meaning for the entire black community.

However, changes in the social, economic, and political landscape of black communities beg for more adequate metaphors to describe the lived experiences of individuals and groups within black churches, particularly those of poor black women. While Paris is certainly correct to describe the historical black church as a surrogate world that provided a sense of refuge for oppressed blacks (particularly during slavery and the beginning years of Reconstruction), many black persons today who live in black communities, including previously incarcerated black men, poor black women, black homosexuals, and black lesbians, may not feel welcomed or understood within these ecclesial communities. In other words, I question whether the Black Church as a surrogate world remains an accurate metaphor to describe how some blacks experience church spaces today.

Womanist scholars such as Delores Williams, Jaquelyn Grant, and Cheryl Townsend Gilkes have called into question whether the Black Church is to be interpreted as a surrogate world or "home" for black women at all. While Paris briefly critiques the church for its overt sexism, some womanist scholars see the Black Church as deeply oppressive for poor black women. In fact, these scholars argue that another image of the Black Church more accurately describes poor black women's church experiences. They describe the Black Church as a "wilderness experience."

In *Sisters in the Wilderness* Williams calls the oppressive life conditions of poor black women a wilderness. Comparing the experiences of African American women to those of the servant Hagar in the Bible, Williams contends that poor black women have often served as sexual and labor surrogates for others. During slavery and the post-bellum period in America, black women were objectified by white male slave masters and their wives, just as Hagar was objectified by Abraham and Sarah. Moreover, black women are oppressed and exploited by black men, particularly within black church contexts. Williams states that "wilderness experience" "is a symbolic term used to represent a near-destruction situation in which God gives personal directions to the believer and thereby helps her make a way out of what she thought was no way."[22]

Williams contends that while black churches "sustain black women emotionally and provide 'theological space' for their expressions of faith," black churches also "suppress and help make invisible black women's thought and culture."[23] Williams argues that black churches have not always been sites of liberation for poor black women. Instead, black churches have often been sites of oppression in which black women have practiced survival, not necessarily liberation. Poor black women as "free" yet "oppressed" speak to the tensions and contradictions many of these women experience within the Black Church.

In fact, black churches are often deeply ambivalent about joining in solidarity with poor black women. Many middle-class black communities do not see themselves as responsible for helping those locked within poor black communities. In fact, the poor are often excluded from liberal and conservative denominational churches. Studies and statistics indicate that the major denominations, including black churches, have memberships that are defined along economic and class lines.[24] Some of the larger black churches in inner cities are constituted of commuting middle-class members who do not feel any sense of responsibility for their inner-city neighbors. Even socially conscious black churches, including those who espouse a social justice rhetoric, fail directly to engage and address problems of poor black women. Even theologies of liberation demonstrate a gap between rhetoric about the preferential option for the poor and actual engagement with the poor.

Ethicist Cheryl Sanders argues that black liberation rhetoric "in the form of statements, resolutions, protests, pickets, and boycotts have failed to engage the poor directly and have little to offer with respect to the practical task of reforming poor communities."[25] In addition, some black churches embrace erroneous cultural images of poor black women, such as welfare queens, blaming them for their own deprivation. As a result, it is not surprising that black church spaces are often experienced as a wilderness for poor black women.

Although some poor black women experience black church spaces as "wilderness" contexts, many black women have nevertheless also seen black churches to be foundational to their sense of religious activism and well-being. We must acknowledge the history of black women's social activism, in which black women have employed their religious efforts to bring about sociopolitical responsibility and racial uplifting.

African American ethicist Rossetta Ross provides a cogent analysis of the ongoing efforts of black women to participate politically on behalf of the black community. Such participation is central to their sense of call and religious duty. Ross is correct that many black women continue to see their religious activism as deeply connected to social problems within black communities.

However, it is important to note that many poor black women are not supported by their black communities to the extent they were several decades ago. As Marcia Riggs rightly observes, black communities have become more fragmented as economic stratification has intensified over the last few decades, contributing to a breakdown in a "black communal consciousness."[26] In order for working class and poor black women to contribute to their communities, more emphasis needs to be given to the types of cultural and economic resources they need to flourish and to become agents of change rather than mythical "superwomen" within their communities.

While black churches do empower some black women to use their religious activism for communal well-being, other black women experience gender oppression within the black churches and are often relegated to the background through celebrations of their "backbone" service.[27] While their persistent and ongoing "backbone" services and efforts have enriched black church life, this reality aggravates persisting sensitivities about the strength and sustainability of black women. Because the typical black church member was and continues to be a working-class black woman (and a large percentage are poor black women), debates about the role that black churches should or should not play in black politics (addressing structural evils) are also implicitly, but rarely explicitly, arguments about the place of black women in American political life. Historically, this sensitivity to the presence and labor of poor black women has been absent in previously noted studies such as those of St. Clair Drake and Horace Cayton's *Black Metropolis*. These studies silenced the majority of church members, who were women.

In the *Black Metropolis*, for example, women and their work were rendered irrelevant to the larger political and intellectual questions at hand, disclosing the patriarchal nature of black scholarship on the significance of black women within churches. Questions must be asked about poor black women's relationship to these institutions. Do black women find themselves contributing their scarce resources to the life of black churches without significant assistance in return? Because black churches have built their buildings as well as their social and cultural programs on poor black women's "pennies," how might black women's thriving relate to their ongoing reality? If black church political participation equates with black women's political participation, what resources might poor black women need to participate effectively in political projects of liberation and flourishing for themselves and their broader communities? Black churches must account for the ways in which black women are affected by black churches' political projects that address structural injustices.

The voices of poor black women are critically important if one is to make normative claims about what the black church has been and what it should be. While it is beyond the scope of this book to take up the absence of black men in black churches, the fact that the majority of black men, unlike their female counterparts, remain outside the churches and their arc of influence remains critically important to the efficacy of black churches in wider society. These questions on the silence of black women and the absence of black men are important in understanding the tensions and ambiguities that continue to characterize black churches in the United States today.

A COMMUNITY OF TRANSCENDENCE

While womanist thinkers are correct in stating that many poor black women experience the black church as wilderness, this image, like the image of a surrogate world, does not fully capture the diverse range of interpretations and meanings of the Black Church today for poor black women. Many black women experience the Black Church in ways that are not captured by either of these metaphors. Some poor black women experience black churches as communities of transcendence that help them make sense of the social worlds in which they are situated. For them, the Black Church is less about being a surrogate world or wilderness and more about how its context enables them to be hopeful despite the contradictions they experience within and without these institutions.

The Black Church as a community of transcendence is not to be associated with the surrogate world image in that it is not a world within a world or an alternative world of sorts. As noted earlier, I doubt whether black communities (as well as some poor black women) continue to see the Black Church as a surrogate world because today's world is characterized by greater class differentiation, sexual differences, and the greater influence of black communal organizations on black political and economic life (black fraternal organizations, black-owned banks, and so on). Instead, some poor black women learn through the Black Church how to make sense of the diverse social worlds they already inhabit. The Black Church gives them ways to make meaning and find fulfillment as they live within their day-to-day contexts of hardship. The Black Church as a community of transcendence captures the Black Church as a complex site of meaning-making (filled with ambiguities and contradictions) for poor black women wherein they may (but do not necessarily) experience life-giving realities such as justice, tenderness, friendship, and communion.

When addressing black women's modes of transcendence, I take up Victor Anderson's notion of transcendence as designating "a dimension of openness within the world of human experience to others, difference, and valuable relationships." Transcendence communicates an experience wherein "virtues of courage, hope, and openness emerge as real possibilities against despair and danger."[28] When Anderson describes his concept of transcendence, he writes that through transcendence

the world is open to novelty. It discloses itself in the interaction and interdependence of all things to each other. It shows itself as proces-

sive, open and relational. Transcendence remains not only a consti-
tutive aspect of the world shared by all, it discloses a felt quality of
religious experience when the self and community transcend isolated
self-interests and seek human fulfillment and flourishing in relation
to larger wholes.[29]

While Anderson is clear that the language of transcendence is not intrinsically theological, it can be interpreted theologically; that is, transcendence
can take on religious meaning.[30] Within the conceptual framework of
poor black women's religious experiences, I refer to transcendence as the
openness of poor black women to ultimate value in the world; it enables
them to act as agents and to make meaning despite debilitating, inhumane
socioeconomic conditions.

By "ultimate value" I mean value that finds its meaning in the idea of
God. While many black women within black churches understand God in
traditional Christian terms, other poor black women may interpret God in
nontraditional ways. For instance, pragmatic theology interprets God as
both an idea and an ideal that provide the ultimate grounding of value and
meaning for all of life. Anderson's pragmatic description of God is helpful. He states, "God is inferentially grasped by reflection on the world, its
processes, patterns, and powers. God gives meaning and value to the whole
of human experience in the world, because God transcends every particular
experience in a unity of experience."[31] He further states, "God signifies the
union of all life in its concrete actuality and ideal potentiality. Therefore,
God designates the infinite in meaning and value."[32] In womanist theology
and ethics the idea of God has been primarily interpreted within Judeo-
Christian categories. However, over the last few years, womanist scholars
such as theologians Monica Coleman and Melanie Harris have made room
for different religious interpretations of God among black women within
black churches and other black religious institutions.[33]

The idea of God does not necessarily need to be understood in strictly
traditional Christian terms. A pragmatic or postmodern notion of God recognizes that nontraditional conceptions of transcendence are as legitimate
as more traditional Christian conceptions of God in empowering these
women to experience courage, hope, and fulfillment within their contexts
of socioeconomic uncertainty and struggle. This more expansive concept
of transcendence enables womanist discourse to stay open to a plurality of
religious experiences as well as the ways in which these women find meaning and ultimate value within their daily lives and contexts of oppression.

Cultural anthropologist Marla Frederick moves beyond notions of the
Black Church as surrogate world or wilderness to themes of transcendence.
In *Between Sundays: Black Women and Everyday Struggles of Faith*, she

explores the political, personal, and spiritual commitments of a group of eight black Baptist women whose experiences have been shaped by the realities of life in a rural, southern community, Halifax County, North Carolina. In these women's lives, spirituality emerges as a space for creative agency, of vital importance to the ways in which these women interpret, inform, and reshape their social conditions that are often characterized by limited access to job opportunities, equitable schooling, and health care. Frederick depicts black church spaces as contexts of transcendence for many of these women. She even remarks on how her role as ethnographer was sometimes secondary as she lived in and among these women, sharing joys, deaths, births, tragedies, and triumphs.[34] Frederick's work seems to infer that many of these women interpret black church spaces as communities of transcendence, empowering them to make meaning within their oppressive circumstances.

Over time, Frederick discovered that these "women's spirituality is less about political dynamics sparked by their faith and more about their cultural identity as black women whose faith in and of itself encompasses the battle against the socioeconomic marginalization they endure."[35] Many of these women of Halifax County have formed grassroots organizations in response to economic woes. However, it is not necessarily some institutional mandate to a "black cause" that motivates and spurs these women to organize grassroots movements. They are motivated instead, it seems, by a creative spirituality that enables them to affirm their own humanity and agency as they develop the political influence to form grassroots organizations in response to the inequities of American political economy. *It is personal transformation and an opportunity for transcendence that these women seek.* Many of these women were able to find opportunities for transcendence in black churches.

This understanding of spirituality among the Halifax County women, as described by Frederick, affirms my claim that there are ways in which the Black Church serves as a community of transcendence. According to Frederick's study, "the idea of spirituality of these women moves beyond notions of an exclusively political and radical black faith; it also allows for what some refer to as desires that may seem 'antithetical to power,' such as love, tenderness, and the search for communion. Their idea of spirituality conveys creativity, the ability to invent, to re-interpret, to move beyond some of the limitations of ritual and static notions of religiosity."[36]

While some poor black women may experience transcendence within black church spaces, I acknowledge that many poor black women remain disillusioned or extremely suspicious of black churches, and this was true of some of the poor black women Frederick interviewed. Lynne, for one, did not trust the institutional life of the black church. Rather, she worked within the Citizens of Tillery, North Carolina (CIT), a community organization that promoted social action related to industrial inequities and other injustices Halifax citizens experienced. For her, the Black Church signified a non-liberative institution that could not address the socioeconomic needs of poor blacks within Halifax. Instead, she turned to community organizations that were directly addressing structural inequities that kept poor black women and children of Halifax in intergenerational cycles of deprivation and poverty. Lynne's subjective experience of black churches is also important in exploring how such institutions might be understood by poor black women.

In part, Frederick's ethnographic study discloses the complexities and ambiguities entailed in the varied, pluralistic experiences of poor black women in relation to black church spaces. Frederick suggests that traditional categories within black church discourse (liberationist or conservative, priestly or prophetic) that could be used to explain poor rural black women's experiences of faith should be rethought in light of their lived experiences of *spirituality*. Moreover, it is important to resist imposing categories on poor black women's realities by turning to their subjective experiences. Finally, Frederick's model also suggests the need for careful readings of the lived experiences of poor black women to see how they make meaning and transcend the debilitating and oppressive sociocultural conditions in which they live.

Frederick's findings do substantiate my suggestion that black churches can be understood as communities of transcendence wherein poor black women find meaning and hope. As stated earlier, describing the Black Church as a community of transcendence avoids the reductivisms of the metaphors of surrogate world and wilderness; it also captures the complexity and diversity of black churches and avoids dualistic language that would seek to pigeonhole these churches into prophetic or priestly, radical or accommodationist.

However, because many black churches understand themselves to be contexts of transcendence for their parishioners, these churches often overlook, underestimate, and/or dismiss larger structural problems that generate and sustain deprivation among poor black women. To be sure, transcendence remains critically important to poor black women's experiences of hope and fulfillment. However, attention to structural obstacles that impede poor black women's sense of flourishing must be addressed, and many anti-poverty strategies within black churches inadequately address these structural dimensions. One of these strategies, faith-based initiatives, will be discussed in the following chapter.

2

Saving Poor Black Women

Faith-Based Initiatives

As a college student I always felt a need to participate in anti-poverty programs within my local church. Specifically, I participated in a food-bank endeavor that involved the donations of canned goods by church members. These canned goods were distributed to a nearby inner-city community. I remember the personal approach that was used in giving these resources to persons in need within this neighborhood. As we talked with different black women who picked up their portion of the resources at a local community center in their neighborhood, I remember the smiles on their faces, eager to see that we cared. I remember young black women talking to me about their aspirations once they were able to achieve financial stability for themselves and their children. Through these conversations I slowly started to sense an inadequacy on our part as a local church community reaching out to these women. While I knew that our actions were very helpful to the immediate survival needs of these women, I sensed that this was a small part of what was needed to empower them toward a more stable socioeconomic future. We were attempting to help them survive and perhaps transcend their own feelings of despair in hopes of a better future. Yet, this didn't address larger systemic concerns that caused them to lose confidence in an economic system that exacerbated their cycle of poverty.

As discussed in the previous chapter, many black churches are contexts of transcendence for poor black women. Yet, larger structural constraints that exacerbate poor black women's conditions of deprivation are left unaddressed. For instance, some black churches employ charitable-choice approaches or faith-based initiatives. While these current approaches to poverty seek to empower these women to find hope and meaning, they fail to address larger structural injustices that perpetuate poverty. Poor black women need to have basic resources necessary for survival and thriving. However, many black churches do not effectively grapple with larger

31

questions of structural injustices and destructive values and ideologies that sustain such injustices.

Black churches currently employ diverse anti-poverty strategies in relation to poor black women. Black churches possess a wide variety of charity-based programs to help struggling black people, particularly women and children. These charity-based ministries include food banks, clothing drives, career services, and more. Such charity-based programs, in part, are current anti-poverty responses within black churches. Moreover, black churches also practice faith-based entrepreneurship that fosters community development projects, giving rise to more entrepreneurial and employment opportunities within poor black communities. In this chapter I explore in depth the charitable-choice strategies or faith-based initiatives because they claim to attack the roots of deprivation and poverty within communities.

Articulated by conservative and liberal camps alike, proponents of faith-based initiatives claim that religious organizations can effectively address poverty and deprivation within communities. However, there continues to be lively discussions over these initiatives. While it is indeed true that faith-based initiatives are able to assist the poor, such as poor black women, such initiatives also operate with assumptions that contribute to the perpetuation of black women's poverty. In critically assessing the assumptions, values, and ideologies that undergird faith-based initiatives, I do not seek to offer a wholesale rejection of these initiatives, nor do I seek to embrace a naive acceptance of them. Instead, I offer a robust assessment of faith-based initiatives, considering their complexities and exploring their range of possibilities and dangers. Most important, I argue that faith-based initiatives fail to consider how issues of the American economy exacerbate black women's deprivation.

OLD BATTLES, NEW DIRECTIONS

The question of faith-based social services initially emerged as a major policy debate in response to the 1996 welfare reform legislation. Under the Clinton administration welfare reform legislation included a central provision known as charitable choice. This provision made it possible for churches and other religious organizations to receive government funds in order to meet the needs of disadvantaged families or at-risk persons within their communities. A central part of the debate concerned whether charitable-choice programs attempt to reform the social welfare system by decentering the Federal Government and placing more responsibility in the hands of state government and local agencies. Later, under the Bush administration, charitable choice was expanded to include an additional set of faith-based initiatives that strengthened the role of religious organizations in public assistance.

Some critics of charitable choice (and eventually faith-based initiatives) argue that social welfare in America has witnessed a revolution as charitable choice radically restructured the relationship between federal government agencies and faith-based service providers. Historically, the welfare-era policy programs unambiguously separated government support from religious benevolence. However, in what some authors refer to as the "post-welfare era" of charitable choice, religious communities and government agencies are seen as partners or allies whose mutual interests can serve the broader goals of public-private well-being. Under charitable choice, religious organizations can seek government funds to underwrite a whole range of social services activities such as job training, childcare, and food assistance. What is important to any discussion of charitable choice is the question of whether it was implemented with an intention to supplant broader governmental welfare programs that ensure support for the most vulnerable members of our society, such as poor women and children.

Critics such as sociologist Barbara Ehrenreich maintain that charitable choice is about religious organizations using the resources of the state to gain more control in order to take over public welfare. She suggests that this measure allows religious entities to govern social assistance by religious directives. In fact, she claims that such legislation "accelerates a downward spiral toward theocracy."[1] She turns to the ways in which right-leaning evangelical churches unapologetically offer proselytizing social services and simultaneously attack candidates who favor the expansion of public services. She concludes that "the evangelical church-based welfare system is being fed by the deliberate destruction of the secular welfare state," placing social welfare at the whims of state officials who can decide the manner in which they will allocate funds for public assistance.[2]

For example, Ehrenreich might argue that charitable-choice and faith-based initiatives have reinforced and exacerbated the moral language surrounding poverty; the language of poverty has been strengthened by religious rhetoric and sensibilities so that being poor is now equated with lacking Christian family values and more. Assumptions and values that blame the poor for their deprivation not only hinder understanding the systemic and cultural factors that adversely affect the poor but also impede cultivating strategies that can ensure a brighter socioeconomic future for the poor. Consequently, Ehrenreich vehemently rejects charitable choice as well as faith-based initiatives, describing these policies as efforts to dismantle the present welfare system.

While I find Ehrenreich's argument somewhat exaggerated (that charitable choice leads to a downward spiral into theocracy), there is some truth in her concerns. For instance, charitable-choice and faith-based initiatives evoke problems surrounding government-funded discrimination. Because faith-based organizations have explicitly religious commitments, can such institutions distribute assistance without religious bias? Charitable choice, then, can obscure the role of church in relation to the state.

The question of fairness of rights also seems to be a legitimate concern in relation to charitable-choice and faith-based initiatives. Implementing faith-based programs when government funding and regulations are involved introduces questions that range from considerations about the rights and fair treatment of clients to considerations about separation of church and state. Criticisms of charitable choice also lift up "questions about recipients' access to agencies capable of meeting their needs without respect to religious preferences, nondiscrimination in supplying services to all qualified applicants, religious tests in hiring agency staff, and the free exercise of religion itself."[3] Providing public funds for religiously based social services providers can potentially reframe how public assistance is understood and practiced, which could adversely affect the people who need public assistance the most.

Without doubt, transitioning social welfare from federal oversight to state oversight with the support of religious communities has radically altered the current social welfare landscape in America. The concern about turning over authority to religious entities raises questions about who bears the responsibility for vulnerable individuals and communities. Because charitable-choice and faith-based initiatives can be interpreted as strategies toward privatization, should public assistance be the sole responsibility of local providers such as faith-based organizations? Or should public assistance be the responsibility of the Federal Government, which could ensure (at least in theory) religious neutrality and fairness in how public assistance is distributed? These questions about responsibility anticipate a larger question surrounding church-state relations when discussing faith-based initiatives: should public provision or private responsibility be privileged in determining programs of public assistance? Faith-based initiatives may imply a struggle between religion-centered methods and governmental, secularist-centered methods in relation to social services.

However, this question of religious-centered versus secular-centered methods in relation to public assistance predates the contemporary debate surrounding faith-based initiatives. Historically, the question on the means and ends of poverty reduction, particularly among women, was not absent in colonial America. The earliest colonial leaders in America accepted the presence of poverty and argued that the obligation to aid the impoverished rested with local communities, not larger governmental institutions. However, poverty continued to be a "growing reality in colonial America as harsh conditions of immigration and settlement left most settlers destitute."[4] As a result, "the first almshouses, also known as poorhouses, were built under church auspices, the first in 1657 in Rensselaerswyck, New York."[5] These particular houses admitted beggars, runaway servants, vagabonds, and impoverished women, who were mostly widowed. Creating poorhouses was a colonial approach to poverty that was grounded in religious-centered methods, particularly when helping the "undeserving" poor.

Religious-centered methods were essential to addressing poverty in early America because "undeserving" persons who needed aid, such as unmarried white women or poor black women (married or unmarried), were seen as immoral and unworthy. In fact, two forms of poverty relief existed in relation to poor women: outdoor relief and indoor relief. Outdoor relief was for "deserving" women (widowed or those whose husbands could not provide). These women received firewood, bread, clothes, medical care, and a small cash payment to care for themselves and their children within the home. Staying within the home was paramount because a woman's moral worth was measured by her ability to fulfill the patriarchal values and norms of homemaking and motherhood. As a result, this type of relief was considered outdoor relief because the funds to help such women went "out" from donor organizations to the women's respective homes.

To the contrary, indoor relief was for "undeserving" unmarried white women or poor black women who did not comply with the patriarchal family ethic of a "true woman." Such "undeserving poor women were forced to work outside the home in exchange for a place in the poorhouse. At the poorhouse they were put to work. Some of these women were even auctioned off and sent out to work in manufacturing settings."[6] At a time when women were expected to confine their productive labor to the home, indoor relief effectively penalized these women for being out of their role.

Poverty relief was controlled primarily by religious organizations and private charities that possessed a religious orientation. Early colonial America did not necessarily see poverty as an issue of personal failure. If one's economic status represented the workings of God, economic need was a natural and inevitable part of the human condition and the well-ordered society. Puritan Calvinism "considered economic rewards to be a sign of predestined grace, and class hierarchies provided an opportunity for the well-to-do to serve society and God by caring for those with less."[7] Hence, providing poverty relief to the impoverished was a religious duty. But this perspective shifted in the nineteenth century.

In the nineteenth century a new paradigm emerged in relation to the provision of public aid. A new explanation of poverty emerged to help justify changes that were occurring. Colonial society had viewed the poor and indigent as unfortunate persons whose poverty was natural and endemic to

l structure, predetermined by God's will; therefore, it merited communal responses. However, the rise of America's market economy created
and privileged new individualistic and moralistic explanations that focused
on the characteristics of the poor. This new paradigm located the problem
of poverty in lack of labor discipline, violations of work ethics, and lack
of family discipline. In other words, poverty was the result of individual
moral failures. Religious-centered methods became essential in correcting
the moral failures of the poor.

This paradigm was carried into the early parts of the twentieth century
as national leaders debated how the "welfare state" should be understood.
The emergence of the modern welfare state threw this historical approach
into question. Initiated by the Great Depression of the early twentieth century, Franklin D. Roosevelt's administration favored the public provision
of relief based on the argument that the problem of poverty had become
too large for private agencies and local communities, and that the public
sector (Federal Government) needed to intervene to provide efficient aid.
With the threatened collapse of the economy, the Social Security Act was
introduced as a federal program to "institutionalize the role of the state in
maintaining families, the labor force, and the general welfare of society."[8]

The Great Depression ushered in a state of chronic crisis within the
economy. It intensified poverty for those already at the bottom and pushed
many working-class families into poverty. Hunger, evictions, perpetual
unemployment and depleted savings disrupted families. Some families fell
apart under the stress and strain of such turmoil. Jobless men frequently
traveled looking for work and, when in despair, deserted their families.
Married women and their children took jobs. Prostitution increased, along
with domestic abuse, malnutrition, alcoholism, desertion, suicide, and starvation. It was a devastating time for America.

Such social, political, and economic conditions prompted leaders to
reassess how welfare assistance should be structured and understood in
America. Should local communities and charities have primary responsibility to assist the poor and needy, or should the state have control of public
assistance? Because of the changing nature of poverty in the twentieth
century, welfare became a function of the modern state. The history on
how poverty has been addressed in America is important. The debate over
whether public assistance should be primarily controlled by the state or
local (religious) communities is *not* a new question. While there are new
aspects to our contemporary crisis concerning poverty and effective anti-
poverty responses, this question has reemerged within our modern political
context, disclosing old battles as well as potentially new directions in the
twenty-first century.

A RETURN TO RELIGIOUS INVOLVEMENT

During the 2000 presidential campaign George W. Bush proffered new policy directions in welfare assistance that hearkened back to the involvement of local communities in solving problems of poverty and deprivation. Once elected, the Bush administration set in motion a number of initiatives to highlight and support the role of religious organizations and communities in providing social welfare. In January 2001, Bush signed an executive order creating and defining the responsibilities of a new agency at the White House for Faith-Based and Community Initiatives. In *Rallying the Armies of Compassion* Bush observed that "federal policy should reject the failed formula of towering, distant bureaucracies that too often prize process over performance." In place of bureaucracies, Bush argued that there should be a partnership between government and private agencies staffed by "quiet heroes [who] lift people's lives in ways that are beyond government's know-how." For Bush, these private charitable groups, including faith-based organizations, were capable of healing the nation's ills "one heart and one act of kindness at a time."[9] Faith-based initiatives were articulated as a compassionate response to those who are poor, destitute, and in need.

A particular assumption grounded the decision of the Federal Government to give religion a more direct role within the social services sector. This assumption was that religious organizations are caring communities that inspire and instill social trust and self-love within recipients, a feat the Federal Government could not readily accomplish.

Proponents of faith-based services argue that religious organizations as caring communities differ from secular service organizations in at least two ways. First, secular social services organizations tend to define relationships between providers and recipients as professionals and clients, whereas being part of a community does not necessarily operate with those rigid distinctions. Second, while relationships between professionals and clients within social services organizations are more likely to consist of arms-length contractual understandings, communities tend to be characterized by shared values, beliefs, understandings, traditions, and norms.[10] Consequently, proponents of faith-based initiatives see religious communities as caring communities that tend to be more efficacious in interacting with persons in need of social services.

Not everyone agrees with the assumption that caring communities automatically are more effective in distributing social services than secular organizations. Opponents of these initiatives contend that religious communities as caring communities may function best by encouraging participants to help other participants rather than by trying to help all who may need aid in the wider community. Moreover, the caring community "may function best by encouraging deep friendships and long-term relationships, rather than by organizing formal programs."[11] However, religious communities as contexts of caring for the needy, particularly for members within that congregational or religious community, should not be confused with the argument that religious communities' value of caring makes them more effective in facilitating formal social services programs for the wider community.

It seems that this debate concerning the capability of religious communities to provide social services is also affected by the ways in which social trust may create positive social services outcomes. Social trust is extremely important to the fabric of societal life. In particular, social trust is extremely important when speaking of social services for lower-income people; social trust can shape this experience to be positive, self-honoring, and culturally respectful.

Social trust also enhances the likelihood of cooperation, which enables people to help others. If people are open to trusting others (at least when that trust is warranted), presumably they will give others the benefit of the doubt when things go wrong, continuing to interact. But if trust erodes, social life can be compromised. Without trust, people become skeptical about the "other." Within the context of social services, when trust is absent, providers remain dubious of recipients and recipients are wary of providers.

The question of the ability of religious communities to sponsor social trust to a greater extent than secular service organizations is paramount. National studies have shown that trust has generally been found to be lower among marginalized populations than among people within privileged groups. Persons with lower incomes are often less likely to express trust than those with higher incomes. In the 2004 General Social Survey, only "about one-quarter of people whose annual income [was] less than $20,000 thought most people could be trusted, compared with about one-third among those with incomes between $20,000 and $30,000 and more than four in ten among those with incomes of $30,000 or more."[12]

A reasonable conclusion is that the people most likely to seek assistance may be predisposed to be distrustful of governmental and secular service providers. As a result, it is particularly important for these organizations to demonstrate their trustworthiness. Recipients of social services often experience a sense of powerlessness when seeking assistance from agencies; in particular, poor black women often experience high degrees of cultural disrespect and powerlessness when dealing with social services agencies, a topic to be discussed in a later chapter. However, Putnam's Social Capital Benchmark Survey in 2000 disclosed that people with low incomes are more apt to trust people or leaders at their churches or places of worship than almost any other target group.[13] As a result, churches are often seen as having a competitive advantage over government-sponsored or secular social services organizations in sponsoring and cultivating social trust.

While faith communities might sponsor social trust, such trust does not necessarily correlate with any increased efficacy of faith-based organizations compared to their secular counterparts. Assessing an organization's effectiveness in carrying out its programs goes further than its ability to sponsor social trust. There are a number of factors that contribute to social services efficacy, and these measurements are continually contested. While issues of assessment in relation to the effectiveness of social services remain debatable, social trust continues to be a major argument for why religious communities as caring communities can be effective in providing social services to disadvantaged persons within their communities.

It also seems reasonable that religious communities understand the stories and narratives of the people they help in ways that a more impersonal service agency does not. For instance, black churches may understand the narratives of deprivation among disadvantaged blacks and have a distinct language for understanding or explaining why such individuals need help. This sense of mutual understanding gives recipients a reason to trust service providers in ways that do not exist within secular organizations. Black churches may possess an interpretive process about how to provide care for the needy within their own congregation or community. Secular social services agencies are less likely to have this type of cultural understanding, which can hinder or complicate the social services relationship between provider and recipient.

Support of the role of religious organizations in providing social welfare is part of a larger debate about the future of civil society. When referring to civil society, I mean a focus on our quality of life together as citizens. It concerns whether or not American citizens are willing to do their part to help one another, and it includes questions about trust and compassion within public life. Within civil society, religion is increasingly seen as a potential resource to address an entire array of social problems such as crime, drugs, poverty, homelessness, and so on. While it is debatable what religious organizations are actually capable of doing to address these social issues within communities, proponents of faith-based initiatives believe that the strengthening of civil society involves religious leadership.

Perhaps what is most intriguing about faith-based initiatives is the underlying assumption that religious communities may be in a better position to "save" the poor, including poor black women. As stated earlier, Bush argued that there should be a partnership between government and private agencies staffed by "quiet heroes [who] lift people's lives in ways that are beyond government's know-how." This statement assumes that religious organizations can offer assistance in ways beyond the scope or ability of the modern state. In other words, religious communities are better positioned to remedy the deprivation of the poor.

DO FAITH-BASED INITIATIVES SAVE POOR BLACK WOMEN?

Many black churches have been proponents of faith-based initiatives and subscribed to the logic and justification for such policies. Black churches are very important institutions in the black community, and many African Americans view their churches as central to their lives. As discussed earlier, during certain historical periods churches were the only important institutions in black communities that were controlled by African Americans themselves. This independence from white society represented a major reason why black ministers played such an important role in the Civil Rights movement. For many black churches faith-based initiatives provide a way to reach out directly to those within their communities who are most vulnerable, extending the legacy of the Civil Rights movement in attending to the needs of the "least of these." These initiatives also enable black churches to present themselves as contexts of transcendence for blacks, especially poor black women. As a result, faith-based initiatives are seen as legitimate responses to black poverty within the context of some black churches.

Political scientist David Bositis did a national study for the Joint Center for Political and Economic Studies entitled "Black Churches and the Faith Based Initiative." This report was conducted between November 11, 2005, and January 24, 2006, and involved 750 black churches. This particular survey highlighted the possibilities that have existed for black churches in relation to faith-based social services. Bositis's study discloses that "while three-fourths of all charitable contributions nationwide went to religious institutions, African Americans contributed nine-tenths of their charitable contributions to churches."[14] Even among congregations in which most members contribute, a large proportion of black churches have limited revenue. Half the churches in this study that provided revenue estimates "had yearly revenue of less than $250,000, and only 12 percent of the churches in the study had yearly revenue in excess of $1 million."[15] Twenty-eight percent had yearly revenue of less than $100,000. In spite of these limited sources of income, many of these churches continue to serve the spiritual and material needs of residents in disadvantaged neighborhoods. Consequently, faith-based initiatives have provided needed revenue sources for black churches that do anti-poverty work.

Furthermore, these black churches often serve communities with substantial needs that cannot be addressed through charitable giving alone. Bositis notes that a large proportion of black churches that serve disadvantaged communities (where faith-based initiative funding is most needed) "do not have the social networks to leverage funding from elsewhere, nor can they leverage extensively from their own congregations."[16] In addition, applying for a faith-based grant requires using and maximizing resources within the church, resources some churches may not have.

In addition, because a number of issues and challenges face African Americans, faith-based initiatives could bring needed funds to help black churches better address these issues at a grassroots level. For instance, according to Bositis: "Black students generally score lower than white students" on standardized tests.[17] Health disparities in communities of color are now recognized as a serious national problem. And according to The Sentencing Project website, "For black males in their thirties, 1 in every 10 is in prison or jail on any given day." While a large number of black churches have social justice ministries that seek to ameliorate these social ills, some black ministers believe that faith-based initiatives could further strengthen these efforts by providing a new funding stream.

However, many pastors (as well as civil rights groups and advocates for the poor) also see many drawbacks to faith-based initiatives. Some black ministers who have doubts or are skeptical of faith-based initiatives express a variety of reasons for their skepticism. Among them were the beliefs that the "government was trying to shift its responsibilities to the church; that involvement with the government was problematic (in part because they believed that acceptance of money from the government led to the loss of the right to criticize it); that the government would insist upon exercising control of their work; and that there were serious issues involving separation of church and state."[18] Some doubted that funds were really available, and others objected to the problem of competition in relation to these funds. Additionally, some ministers said that they were not interested "because the application process was too cumbersome or they lacked the technical capacity to participate."[19]

Finally, while a majority of black ministers approve of and would like to participate in faith-based initiatives, serious challenges do face smaller churches and churches with limited revenues. It is clear that "even the larger and wealthier black churches need legal advice and help with paperwork, policy information, the formation of collaborative programs, and program evaluations," while the needs of smaller and (especially) rural black churches are even greater (so much so that many are not interested in participating because they believe that they lack the capabilities to apply).[20]

As noted earlier, churches need to invest or leverage resources in order to complete an application for faith-based funding, and some may even need to overhaul their administrative structure once they receive the funding. It is likely that smaller churches do not have these resources and do not know how to network in order to leverage them from sources outside the congregation. In short, they not only have limited resources, but they are also embedded in a very limited network. Interestingly, Bositis's study reveals that many black churches are at a distinct disadvantage when applying for these funds. Consequently, many black churches are unable to take advantage of available federal grants because of their limited resources. Bositis's national study on faith-based social services programs and black churches illuminates many of the real benefits and drawbacks that black ministers associate with faith-based initiatives.

Undoubtedly, faith-based initiatives offer real possibilities for black churches that do social services work and have limited financial support. Nonetheless, faith-based initiatives do not address larger systemic issues that exacerbate black women's poverty. Moreover, faith-based initiatives possess particular destructive assumptions about poor black women, namely, that these women are in need of moral reformation in order to improve their socioeconomic conditions. In fact, within the idea of charitable-choice and faith-based initiatives, poor mothers tend to be generally represented as a kind of moral recovery project for the churches as well as for the state.

A common theme within some black churches is that economic poverty is really a reflection of spiritual poverty. The senior leader of New Covenant Life Church, Pastor John Marsh, reinforces this theme when he describes the startling poverty in his area as a "spiritual issue." He recounts helping at a homeless shelter and realizing that poverty was not economic but spiritual. He states:

> When people have rejected God, or perhaps when they have no truth that's ever been taught them about how to really relate to God through faith in the Lord Jesus and the power of the Holy Spirit, they are going to look to something else, and that something else could be drugs or it could be the occult or some other destructive thing that ruins relationships and can ruin health and basically makes havoc of the human person.[21]

From this pastor's perspective, poverty can be effectively addressed only when people are "drawn into a life-transforming experience of a faith community."[22] This description of poverty as a spiritual ailment continues to obscure discussion within black communities and black churches on the problem of poverty.

Similarly, Glenn Loury, an African American economist, invoked the need for black churches to instill values in poor black women when he testified during the 1995 congressional hearings that prepared the way for welfare reform's law of charitable choice. Loury advocated the restoration of moral teaching in black communities to help stem the tide of "illegitimacy problems and family breakdown." Loury argued that the structure of the single, black female-headed family had to change or black families would continue to threaten "the survival of the republic."[23] He argued that necessary moral guidance could occur through religious institutions. Because he identified these institutions as the leading and most important source of help, he suggested that financial aid be sent directly to churches so that these women and girls could learn to change their lives.

Political leaders have also identified black churches as central to poor black women's moral reformation and improved economic chances. Black feminist and social ethicist Traci West describes a speech that President Clinton gave in 1995 to the Progressive National Baptists, a predominantly black Protestant denomination. West notes that President Clinton sought the support and participation of these church leaders in his welfare reform agenda by linking the entire problem of poverty to teenage mothers.[24]

In his speech Clinton posited that black religious leaders could help cut the poverty rate by more than 50 percent if they could help black female teenagers who are unmarried to not have babies. In part, Loury's and Clinton's speeches were used to argue a particular point in relation to black women's poverty: that black religious institutions such as black churches should be seen as primary institutional agents that instill Christian family values in order to "fix" or "solve" black women's deprivation. An underlying assumption was that if poor black women undergo a transformation of values or moral reformation, their socioeconomic circumstances will improve, if not be solved.

Like Clinton, President George W. Bush operated with the same assumptions as he touted both his 2004 Healthy Marriage Initiative and Faith-Based Initiative bill, extensions of the charitable choice legislation. In 2003, Bush gave a speech to a group of Christian leaders in which he affirmed the key role of the church in meeting the needs of the poor. He stated, "Welfare policy will not solve the deepest problems of the spirit." He noted, "You don't fix the crack in the wall until you fix the foundation."[25] President Bush's comments reflect the viewpoint that people who lack socioeconomic resources, such as poor black women, need assistance because their "foundation" is cracked.[26] Moreover, Bush's viewpoint assumes that churches are better positioned to address this "foundational" moral problem in the poor. Moreover, when praising his Healthy Marriage Initiative's policy for the poor, one White House aide told the press, "The president loves to do that sort of thing in the inner city with black churches, and he's very good at it."[27]

Undoubtedly, many benefits accrue to churches that choose to partner with state programs such as welfare reform or charitable choice. The exposure to media attention and the status of publicly receiving approval from the seat of power lures many of these churches to cooperate with such programs, including perhaps their distorted assumptions about poor black women. In fact, the aforementioned study by Bositis echoes this concern among some black ministers. They want to make sure that they are able to retain their autonomy to critique unjust institutions and practices; others are concerned about losing their prophetic voice. They want to fulfill their perceived obligation in not only speaking truth to power but also confronting injustice and suffering wherever they see it.

Ideologies that hold poor black women to be personally irresponsible inform the ways black churches address poverty within their communities. For instance, Kirby John Caldwell's Windsor Village UMC complex of nonprofits in Houston, Texas, is partly funded by faith-based initiatives. The website for Windsor Village UMC and its affiliated nonprofits, kingdombuilder.com, describes the group as "The Power Connection." Within the Power Connection are nine nonprofit organizations that are dedicated to addressing the "elements that affect the human condition." In particular, Ujima is the faith-based organization that serves disadvantaged communities in the Houston area. Eighty percent of the families served by Ujima live at or below the poverty line as welfare recipients and are unemployed or under-employed.

One immediately notices that the language of self-help and individual responsibility pervades the description of this faith-based organization. The website states, "Critical factors of our success have been achieved through the development of high moral values, promotion of health and positive self-images, building of strong educational foundations, endorsement of family unity, provision of economic opportunities, and the fostering of community advocacy." It continues, "Our services consist of six key components designed to empower participants to assume active responsibility for their lives and make significant steps and progress toward the attainment of their goals and visions."

While these pronouncements to empower poor blacks to pursue their goals and develop positive self-esteem are not negative or unworthy programmatic aims, it is problematic that committed discussions on how systems impede their aims from being actualized are completely absent. Moreover, these pronouncements tend to reinforce the market-driven language of individual success and responsibility, blaming the poor for their condition. Such self-help language that grounds faith-based initiatives does not help poor black women; instead, it is complicit with the institutions or programs that fuel distorted discourses surrounding the nature of poverty itself.

Approaches such as faith-based initiatives that treat poverty as curable through individual responsibility and positive moral behavior reflect certain neo-liberal ideologies and political projects within the United States. John Bartkowski and Helen Regis's *Charitable Choices* explores how the logic of faith-based initiatives relates faith communities to the poor as communities of moral formation that aid the poor in developing the type of values that lead out of poverty. Advocates of faith-based initiatives call special attention to the repository of resources within faith communities (for example, high moral integrity, close-knit relationships among co-religionists, and so on). These resources are seen as giving religious communities a unique role in assisting the poor. As a result, champions of these initiatives believe that religious organizations are superior providers of social services because of the moral values they embody and the holistic goals to which they aspire. While these resources are not bad in themselves, the assumption that these resources are necessary because of the moral failures of the poor is faulty and dangerous.[28]

In critically assessing assumptions, values, and ideologies that undergird faith-based initiatives, I do not seek to offer a wholesale rejection of the charitable-choice legislation. Nor do I seek to embrace a naive acceptance of it. Instead, I feel it is essential to assess these faith-based initiatives, exploring the range of possibilities and dangers in relation to such policies. When turning to black churches that employ faith-based initiatives such as Kirby's Windsor Village, it is obvious that these strategies seek to empower poor black women to transcend their socioeconomic miseries as well as to find meaning and hope in order to improve their lives. However, and as noted before, there is a danger when this *excludes* a systemic critique of the structures that may impede poor black women's sense of flourishing, or when neo-liberal values and assumptions are unacknowledged within the framework of these approaches.

While not within the purview of this chapter, I do want to note that black faith-based entrepreneurship has also gained ground as a complex contemporary response to black women's poverty. Similar to charitable-choice and faith-based initiatives, black faith-based entrepreneurship desires to aid black women's sense of flourishing and well-being despite their circumstances, although it simultaneously reinforces a philosophy of individual success. As mentioned earlier, T. D. Jakes challenges black women to dream big and act courageously, employing greater personal agency toward their life goals and objectives. He encourages black women to be more assertive and decisive in accomplishing their dreams. He attempts to persuade black women that their dreams matter and that they should invest in their future in order to make a difference in their own lives and the lives of others. While this message in itself is quite inspiring, one is left wondering about the dangers of such a message when there is not a parallel critique of structures that impede these women as well as a challenge to existing neo-liberal values that support structural injustices.

Many black churches that employ faith-based initiatives (as well as faith-based entrepreneurship) genuinely desire to aid poor black women to embrace hope and confidence in what is possible through their own efforts and actions. However, poor black women's possibilities toward self-actualization are weakened if serious attention is not given to *why* these women are continually locked in cycles of intergenerational deprivation and poverty. Such cycles of deprivation result from more than these women's lack of effort to succeed. These cycles of poverty are grounded in the larger issues of American political economy. Only by understanding the underlying causes of the situations of deprivation experienced by poor black women can black churches understand the dangers of such initiatives and think critically about how to address structural inequities.

While the Black Church is riddled with tensions, complexities, and ambiguities, it is also a site that has tremendous potential to transform cultural inequalities that stigmatize poor black women as deviant. It has tremendous potential to provide a context out of which poor black women can flourish. While many black churches have desired to be communities of transcendence for poor black women through faith-based initiatives, many black churches have not been effective in addressing the systemic nature of the economic inequalities poor black women face in the twenty-first century. In order to participate effectively in the project of hope and thriving for and with poor black women, black churches must understand the increasing significance of an American underclass and the experiences of poor black women within this underclass.

3

We Too Are America

Black women continue to contribute to the economic, social, and political landscape of this country. However, black women (particularly poor black women) are often treated like second-class citizens because of inequitable structures and practices. Consider this fact: although poor black women are seen as lazy and not desirous of work, impoverished black women have a long history of strong participation in the labor force. Consider this fact: although black women are seen as the "face" of poverty, the overwhelming group of impoverished persons remains white (although black women are disproportionately represented). Consider this fact: poor black women along with other poor persons across racial groups continue to experience a lack of a living wage, healthcare, childcare, and more, which exacerbates their cycles of deprivation.

While these facts are generally acknowledged among sociologists and political scientists, the mythological narrative of poor black women as the cause of poverty in America retains its currency within our society. This erroneous narrative not only drives how we discuss poverty within our nation but also informs how we craft policy for the poor (such as faith-based initiatives that place the amelioration of poverty in the moral reformation of poor black women). Black churches must respond to this dilemma. All black religious institutions must examine and address the real economic inequities poor black women face today.

But before black churches respond to this dilemma, they must grasp that black women's current experiences of poverty have changed as economic shifts have created an American underclass in the last four decades. Racial injustice as the dominant explanation of black poverty must change. This chapter contends that racism exists, but it alone does not explain the economic opportunities and realities of poor black communities, and particularly poor black women. Class does matter. The dominant tendency of black national leaders has been to subordinate arguments about class to broader discussions about race in relation to black poverty. This simply will not work if black churches are to address adequately black impoverishment within this nation.

Black churches would do well to cultivate political wisdom on contemporary problems of black poverty in order to counteract assumptions that often accompany their anti-poverty strategies such as charitable choice approaches. Such cultivation of political wisdom first involves acknowledging the new forms of economic inequities that poor black women experience that do not put them on a "level playing field" with middle-class and upper-class persons, including middle- and upper-class black persons.

This wisdom also involves acknowledging that there are multiple black Americas. The oppressive experiences of poor black women are qualitatively different from middle- and upper-class black communities. Consequently, race cannot be seen as the sole determinant of these women's opportunities. Instead, poor black women's experiences of poverty can be grasped and understood more adequately by exploring historical shifts in American political economy and how these shifts intensify and worsen their experiences of deprivation. In other words, class matters.

Since the Reagan administration in the 1980s, state decisions related to economic policy have been guided by a free-market ideology and the accompanying neo-liberal interests that reinforce economic deprivation and social alienation for the poor of racial affiliations. This chapter explores major shifts in the American political economy from the 1960s onward that adversely affect persons across all races, producing a black underclass within a larger American underclass. This chapter also spells out the unique conditions poor black women face, which exposes the real power interests associated with a free-market ideology. Before turning to these historical shifts that have exacerbated intergenerational cycles of poverty among blacks in the twenty-first century, I briefly discuss a particular ideology that drives the destructive side of free-market forces in America.

CRITIQUE OF FREE-MARKET IDEOLOGY AND ITS NEO-LIBERAL INTERESTS

Free-market ideology contends that persistent poverty within black communities is due to a pathological black culture whose attitudes, behaviors, practices of crime, teenage pregnancy, devaluing of education, promiscuity, and so forth perpetuate impoverishment and lack of attainment. This free-market ideological reading of black poverty as due to black cultural deficiencies is grounded in an understanding of free-market fundamentalism that finds its greatest expression in Milton Friedman's *Capitalism and Freedom*. Friedman's capitalist "manifesto" was written in the 1960s at the height of the social welfare reforms that were being formulated by President John F. Kennedy and later instituted by Lyndon Baines Johnson's progressive liberal agenda. Friedman addressed a particular question that created great contestation between free-market advocates and welfare-state promoters during President Johnson's Great Society, and this was the question of the role of government within market activity. Friedman argued that the role of government inhibited and vitiated economic efficiency when intervening in market activity with paternalistic social welfare policies that largely did not achieve their intended goals and effects.

Friedman's Belief in a Free-Market Economy

For Friedman, the logic of free-market economy is based on four uncontested assumptions: (1) the market and the government are discrete entities that should be left to their own internal mechanisms; (2) the market contains its own laissez-faire morality, which grants success to individuals who work hard; (3) freedom in economic arrangements is itself a component of freedom broadly; and (4) economic freedom is also an indispensable means to the achievement of political freedom.[1] These four assumptions, for Friedman, can be effective only when government plays a minimal role in free-market activity. The state should simply be a "rule maker" (setting rules of engagement for market sectors) and "umpire" (being a whistle-blower, for example, on monopolies that adversely inhibit competitive capitalism and hence economic freedom). The state should not be paternalistic because it thwarts the market's self-sufficient, internal mechanisms that ensure the actualization of citizens' freedoms and liberties through the market.

For Friedman, the supreme value of free-market activity is the maximization of economic and political freedom based on one of free-market's central principles: voluntary and informed market exchange. In economic transactions, both parties enter the transaction voluntarily in order to benefit mutually from the exchange. Because of this voluntary exchange, Friedman asserts that "this exchange brings about coordination without coercion."[2] For him, the hallmark of each economic transaction within free-markets is that it allows for political and economic freedom without infringing upon individual rights and liberties. Consequently, he maintains that free-market logic entails within it the condition of freedom for all members of society, which dismisses any need for the government to regulate (or intervene within) economic activity in pursuit of these freedoms.

When addressing discrimination within the market or claims that the market inhibits minority group's freedoms, Friedman contends that the free-market "separates economic efficiency from irrelevant characteristics such as discrimination of color or religion."[3] He implies that economic factors such as efficiency always drive the economic human, never noneconomic factors that could decrease a person's efficiency. Friedman writes:

No one who buys bread knows whether the wheat from which it is made was grown by a Communist or a Republican, by a constitutionalist or a Fascist, or, for that matter, by a Negro or a white. This illustrates how an impersonal market separates economic activities from political views and protects men from being discriminated against in their economic activities for reasons that are irrelevant to their productivity—whether these reasons are associated with their views or their color.[4]

He suggests that non-economic variables (such as racial bias or religious prejudice) do not affect economic exchanges because of their negative effects on economic efficiency, which rational economic actors would refuse. As a result, Friedman maintains that economic inequity and inequality, if they arise, "should be resolved through appealing to the rational economic actor in terms of the ways in which such prejudiced behavior leads to economic inefficiency."[5]

Moreover, Friedman asserts that social welfare responses to inequality and inequity represent the greatest circumscription of freedoms because these welfare responses advocate a paternalistic role for government in matters of poverty. He contends that paternalism is inevitable for those whom we designate as "not responsible." Within this claim, Friedman explicitly correlates poor people who are recipients of social welfare programs with those who are irresponsible. He gives an example of public housing and asks why the government does not simply "give low-income participants a lump sum of money to purchase the housing they need instead of paternalistically providing subsidized housing."[6] He responds that government is inadvertently admitting that "families being helped 'need' housing more than they 'need' other things but would themselves either not agree or would spend the money unwisely."[7] Hence, for Friedman, the logic of social welfare programs expresses a direct link between these programs and representations of the poor as personally irresponsible.

However, Friedman's "uncontested assumptions," which seem natural and "given" within his free-market reasoning, contain particular interests. Foremost, Friedman's claim that the market sponsors voluntary, non-coercive exchange, in fact, does not account for the real imbalances of authority and power that are features of much market-exchange activity. For example, an employee might choose to exchange her labor for wages that do not bring her above the poverty-level line. In this situation, Friedman's logic dismisses how the employer's authority to hire hundreds of applicants who are vying for a job can create a hegemonic reality wherein the employee is influenced (against her interests due to job security) to accept the employer's exploitative job conditions and standards. In this case, market-exchange activity is fraught with ambiguity wherein consent may not negate the presence of hegemonic attitudes and actions between parties; instead, such activity expresses manipulative power relations. The assumption that free-market activity is physically non-coercive and therefore voluntary does not address the question of hegemony, which allows economic elites to maintain the status quo of excessive economic profit at the expense of low-income workers.

In light of this case, Friedman's other claims that the free-market has its own discrete self-correcting, internal mechanisms and its own laissez-faire morality that rewards merit and hard work are also guided by the interests of economic elites in America. In the United States, the Wall Street financial crisis of 2008 is an example of the problems of governmental deregulation of our free-market economy. Because the federal government embarked on a series of deregulation policies during the Reagan administration, the financial markets were "free to set mortgage terms and interest rates that proved to be exploitative to American homeowners."[8] While mortgage banks claimed that they sought to provide greater access to homeownership to the American public, many mortgage loan companies intentionally provided loans to American families at interest rates that they knew these families over time would be unable to repay, which predicted greater profit for the mortgage companies.

Clearly, mortgage companies possessed instrumental interests in loaning such money for housing to American families. The debt of American families benefitted many financial elites. However, the mortgage and financial companies miscalculated their profit predictions and instead experienced financial failure and ruin alongside millions of families. Friedman's belief in the free-market possessing its own internal mechanisms is belied by the series of governmental deregulation policies that created the greatest financial crisis since the Great Depression of the 1930s.

Friedman's additional claim that laissez-faire morality ensures success based on merit conceals the interests of the very wealthy in how success is attained within the United States. Success is often not based on the efforts, talents, and merits of people. For instance, persons may attain economic and social success based on inheritance or ancestry. Others receive economic and sociopolitical benefits based on their membership in an elite group or club that enables achievement and success. Friedman does not consider the critical force of power relations in determining groups who are born into affluence and those who seemingly are born outside of such privileged arrangements and opportunities. Economic and social privilege contradicts a free-market economy whose rewards are based on merit. The powerful interests attached to notions of meritocracy within free-market ideology conceal the way in which socioeconomic privilege undermines parity among the members of a society, systematically excluding the less fortunate.

D'Souza's Application of Friedman

A final problem associated with Friedman's free-market ideology is the direct correlation that Friedman makes between social welfare programs and the "irresponsible" poor. Such representations of poor persons as moral failures conceal how economic structures and practices impede opportunity and access, which thwarts the ability of poor persons to thrive and flourish. In particular, a more contemporary political scientist, Dinesh D'Souza, applies Friedman's neo-liberal logic of cultural deficiencies and personal moral failure in relationship to poor black communities.

Following Friedman's free-market logic, D'Souza articulates a thesis of "cultural deficiencies" and "personal failure" in explaining the causes of economic failure within poor black communities. He argues that the fundamental causes of black poverty are the cultural deficiencies and pathologies of black cultural life. He contends that

> the last few decades have witnessed nothing less than a breakdown of civilization within the African American community. This breakdown is characterized by extremely high rates of criminal activity, by the normalization of illegitimacy, by the pre-dominance of single-parent families, by high levels of addiction to alcohol and drugs, by a parasitic reliance on government provision, by a hostility to academic achievement, and by a scarcity of independent enterprises.[9]

D'Souza defines the crisis of black impoverishment as a breakdown of "productive values" needed for excellence in all spheres of life. D'Souza implies that this breakdown of values has its origins in "a defective history of slavery and racism that blacks continue to employ in naming their own victimization."[10]

D'Souza believes that "attributing black poverty to white racism deflects criticism of these cultural deficiencies that impede black progress and attainment."[11] He identifies black culture as an "oppositional culture" that rejects the "white man's worldview." He posits that such a worldview is equated with values of education, family values, entrepreneurship, and more. The black oppositional culture is characterized by pathological behavior and values, impeding black people's well-being in a competitive and technological society. D'Souza claims that perpetually blaming the white perpetrator for the dysfunctional and destructive patterns of black victims does not give these victims help in relation to their economic problems. Moreover, he argues that blacks use racism as an excuse to not be responsible in the competitive, market-driven society in which we live. He posits, "Another problem is that by focusing almost entirely on the cause of pathologies, excuse theorists offer no coherent vision about what to do about them."[12]

However, D'Souza's cultural deficiencies argument is flawed and dishonest about the context in which poor blacks often find themselves. He traces black cultural pathology to "deficiencies," without giving a historical, systematic account of the causes of these deficiencies. Offering a "coherent vision about what to do about deficiencies" requires that the underlying causes that are producing these deficiencies be adequately explored.

While D'Souza attempts to show that black poverty exists primarily because blacks (as well as "experts" in racial apologetics) continue to exploit racist excuses, he never considers how structural factors adversely affect poor black communities. D'Souza doesn't ask how *economic* structures and systems disempower poor black communities, in which poor black women are a large percentage. His analysis is isolated from social oppression and exclusion, the conditions that foster poverty and wealth, and broader historical circumstances. Black poverty is not about the "abilities," "excuses," or "behaviors" of a culture, but about an economic system that continues to impose structural disadvantages on poor blacks.

Moreover, D'Souza incorrectly maintains that blacks' intellectual abilities are substandard to whites and Asians as demonstrated by blacks' low levels of academic achievement. He does not acknowledge that a major barrier to intellectual achievement as well as employment prospects and productivity is being able to purchase quality education. Intellectual and academic achievements are also conditioned by family structure and the quality of socioeconomic resources devoted to ensuring success. D'Souza does not take into account the long history of economic disenfranchisement that has not only severely crippled poor blacks but also stagnated poor whites.

Similar to Friedman's arguments, those of D'Souza's are connected to the power interests of economic elites that conceal the practices of a post-industrial political economy and its absence of structural opportunities for the poor, including poor black women. A history of shifts in the American political economy has left behind a group of unskilled labor, which has affected a disproportionate number of blacks (particularly in the inner city). Yet, by blaming the victims, economic elites that benefit and amass wealth from such structures are able to deflect attention from the need for the radical reform and restructuring of the American political economy. Moreover, by persuading the masses that the poor are morally culpable (based on free-market assumptions of fairness and parity), economic elites are able to maintain the immutability and inviolability of these economic arrangements. Consequently, blaming poor blacks (and in particular, poor black women) hides the real economic experiences of a black underclass that continues to suffer. But what are the economic experiences of a black underclass? And what *is* a black underclass?

MULTIPLE BLACK AMERICAS

There is no such thing as a Black America with unified interests and needs. Yet, both black and white leaders perpetuate this myth. Pulitzer Prize–winning writer Eugene H. Robinson persuasively argues that the African American population has splintered into four distinct and increasingly disconnected entities: a small elite with enormous influence, a mainstream middle-class majority, a newly emergent group of recent immigrants from Africa and the Caribbean, and an abandoned minority "with less hope of escaping poverty than at any time since Reconstruction's end."[13] Drawing on census records, polling data, sociological studies, and his own experiences growing up in a segregated South Carolina college town during the 1950s, Robinson explores 140 years of black history in America, focusing on how the Civil Rights movement, desegregation, and affirmative action contributed to the fragmentation. Of particular interest is his discussion of how immigrants from Africa, the "best-educated group" coming to live in the United States, are changing what being black means. Robinson notes that despite the enormous strides African Americans have made in the past forty years, the problems of poor blacks remain as intractable as ever.

While white racism impedes poor blacks, class division and exploitation are present within black communities, profoundly contributing to the deprivation of poor blacks. Activities of the black elite from Reconstruction to the present often reinforce the process of capital accumulation as well as the exploitation of the poor black masses. Historically, the black elite has occupied four primary vocations: politicians, clergymen, educators, and entrepreneurs.[14] Of these four occupations, the black entrepreneurs or black capitalists have been used to reinforce certain forms of market exploitation experienced by a black underclass. Black capitalists perpetuate two key dilemmas that further subjugate poor blacks. First, because they must depend on a larger American capitalist system, black capitalists tend to feel forced to subscribe to the capitalist mentality of profitability at any cost. Second, the profit mentality of black capitalists has led to further exploitation of the black consumer market.

The Negative Effects of Black Capitalism

Black capitalism is a term that originated during the Reconstruction era and was rekindled during the Reagan administration in the 1980s. It was first argued by W. E. B. Du Bois, and taken up again by black leaders during Reagan's administration, that black capitalism would cultivate the economic development of the black community. Propertied black people would start businesses and accumulate capital in order to create job opportunities for the unemployed black masses. This accumulation of capital within black communities would then contribute to the advancement and racial empowerment of all black people. This solution to black people's plight was praised by W. E. B. Du Bois during the era of Reconstruction and oftentimes uncritically lauded by such activists as Thomas Sowell at the outset of Reagan's administration. Yet, the solution of black capitalism often participates in free-market oppression because black capitalists often thrive by exploiting the black consumer market.

Black capitalists often must compete and be complicit with white corporate strategies that focus on the exploitation of a consumer market, in this case, black consumers. The general corporate strategy is to increase profitability at the expense of the consumer. It is generally recognized that urban poor and lower-income consumers pay much higher prices than affluent white suburbanites for commodities, as long as sufficient lines of credit are made available to them. Unfortunately, "almost two-thirds of all poor blacks buy their household appliances either exclusively or primarily on credit, often on terms that exceed market credit rates by over 100 percent."[15] Black capitalists must deal with the class-conscious propaganda that is created by white corporations (and advertisers) to secure poor black consumerism.

In order to achieve profitability, black capitalists often collude with capitalist advertising strategies and financial practices that exploit race. In 1971, "when Schieffelin and Company, manufacturers of Teacher's Scotch, learned that black people per capita consumed 50 percent more scotch than whites, it created a film narrated by Jesse Owens."[16] Called *The Black Athlete*, this film was shown in every US city with a large black consumer market. "Teacher's Scotch Sports Night" was arranged by black liquor salesmen. Moreover, this film was "shown in bars in smaller black communities and in black public libraries."[17] Within their own communities today, black business owners of payday loan shops often charge exorbitant, exploitative interest rates on loans, as much as 400 percent. These are examples of how black capitalists and the black elite have often functioned as a "middleman presence" for American economic institutions, often resulting in the exploitation of poor blacks. This tension between poor blacks and middle- to upper-class black capitalists complicates any discussion on how race and class affect black persons in America.

The Importance of Class

Class injustice matters to the lives of poor blacks, and class structures the opportunities of poor blacks in qualitatively different ways from those of middle- to upper-class blacks. Sociologist William Julius Wilson asserts that class has become as important as race in determining black opportunities in the modern industrial period. He argues that "in the economic realm . . . the black experience has moved historically from economic racial oppression experienced by virtually all blacks to economic subordination for the black underclass."[18] This predicament of poor blacks cannot be singularly addressed by the passage of civil rights laws or the introduction of special racial programs such as affirmative action. Indeed, as Wilson maintains,

> the very success of recent anti-discrimination efforts in removing racial barriers in the economic sector only points out, in sharp relief, other barriers that create greater problems for some members of the black population than for others; such barriers transcend the issue of racial ethnic discrimination and depict the universal problems of class subordination.[19]

Modern economic shifts have engendered a black underclass phenomenon that cannot be described merely as a result of racial oppression but, rather, as a result of the universal problems of class inequalities and inequities. This problem of class subordination as central to the opportunities of a black underclass is critical to obtaining justice for poor blacks. *Racial programs alone will not solve a black underclass dilemma. Rather, policies and practices that aim at structural changes in economic institutions for the poor of all races are central to thriving for this underclass.*

The articulation of complex class analysis and economic history from the 1970s onward must begin with a disclosure of what is at stake for a black underclass. Class is of increasing importance in the analysis of the sources and causes of poverty among blacks; however, I do not interpret this discussion of the black underclass in terms of a race vs. class debate. Rather, I seek to reinterpret critically this debate, noting that race and class constitute two factors (among other factors such as gender, sexuality, age, and so on) that uniquely structure the opportunities of a black underclass in a qualitatively different way than that of blacks in the upper and middle classes.

To be sure, *black underclass* has been a controversial term within black feminist and womanist discourses. Economist and educator Teresa Amott has problematized the sexist connotations that the term communicates. Amott contends that these poor, black, single mothers in a so-called black underclass are not presented as "agents of their own lives."[20] She notes that black women have "survived and created meaning and dignity" as single mothers even though social policies in this country have been hostile to such non-nuclear families. These women "do not construct their lives as half of a male-breadwinner, female-homemaker pair, but rather they see their roles as *single* mothers as central to their own lives."[21] Amott maintains that "black underclass" does not account for black women's agential capacities. She is concerned that the language of underclass identifies poor black women as "pathological" and victims of racist, sexist, and classist oppressions without showing how poor black women subvert institutional and organizational forms of exploitation and discrimination. Consequently, the discourse on a black underclass could "potentially further exacerbate the objectification of black women as non-agential beings."[22] For Amott, the term *black underclass* attaches moral guilt to impoverished blacks and fails to capture the resiliency and agency of poor black women.

I do not employ the language of the underclass in a pejorative way. My usage of "underclass language," like Wilson's, is intended to emphasize the economic significance (rather than moral significance) of detailing the structural problems within the American political economy that forces poor blacks into intergenerational cycles of poverty and deprivation. The language of underclass is an articulation of the plight of poor blacks who suffer from marginalization within a larger post-industrial economy. Wilson states that the underclass is a "heterogeneous grouping of families and individuals who are outside the mainstream American occupational system."[23] The underclass includes individuals who lack training and skills as well as those who experience long-term unemployment (who often become welfare dependent) and/or are engaged in street crime. This term signifies a group of people who "have been left behind" economically and socially.[24]

The term *black underclass* is meant to communicate the experience of social and economic alienation among poor blacks that creates *permanent*, intergenerational cycles of deprivation and poverty. The systemic oppression of poor blacks has ramifications in terms of social disorganization within urban and rural areas. The language of underclass is not intended to convey cultural and personal moral failures of poor blacks. Rather, the term *underclass* conveys the structural flaws within American economic systems and social institutions that have created, perpetuated, and exacerbated poverty among black communities.

Underclass also suggests a group of persons who do not experience the conditions that make class standing possible. Within classical Marxist class analysis, class standing presumes that persons participate in both the division of labor and modes of production.[25] The black underclass suffers from four basic conditions that do not make class standing possible for them: (1) they are chronically underemployed and/or *unemployed*, (2) they are minimally or under educated, (3) they are usually over incarcerated, and (4) they are often homeless.[26] The shift in the American economy in the late 1960s onward led to chronic unemployment and a structural absence of opportunities for poor blacks, particularly in urban areas. This shift in the larger American political economy intensified the poverty of blacks. Consequently, these four basic conditions that many poor blacks suffer from became intergenerational features. Briefly, when referring to a black underclass, I am describing how our American post-industrial political economy creates and fosters these four basic conditions that determine class standing for many poor blacks today.

In addition, it is important to note that the language of a black underclass communicates the dread, fear, hopelessness, and disappointment that often accompany a lack of class standing in America. While black feminists and womanists have attempted to highlight poor black women as agents, they have often downplayed the real existential despair that pervades underclass communities because of their experiences of economic and social alienation and abandonment within the American economy. As a result, my use of *black underclass*: (1) refers to a black population that is not incorporated into basic conditions that make class standing possible; (2) takes seriously the dread, disappointment, hopelessness, and despair that often accompany underclass communities; and (3) accounts for poor black women's agency in discussions of poverty and exploitation. When reviewing the real presence of class injustices for poor blacks, multiple black Americas become more visible.

HISTORICAL SHIFTS TOWARD A POST-INDUSTRIAL POLITICAL ECONOMY

Poor black women continue to experience conditions that complicate their gaining class standing. Neo-liberal assumptions and values concerning the moral bankruptcy of these women result in conclusions that are both untrue and misleading. Because poor black women within a black underclass experience deprivation due to inequitable economic institutions and practices, middle- to upper-class blacks must be careful not to frame the impoverishment of these women solely in terms of race. Race alone cannot be seen as the determinant of black poverty. Economist Marcellus Andrews describes the American underclass phenomenon as not simply a distinctively "black problem." Andrews argues that racism abets the more basic problem of class inequalities among poor black communities because of the shift in the structure of the American economy toward a knowledge-and-technology driven system that offers huge rewards to brains over brawn, [which adversely affects most of the poor regardless of race] because they remain an industrial labor force in a post-industrial country.[27] Because a wider post-industrial political economy is a knowledge-based and technologically driven economy, the most qualified must have access to quality education.

This post-industrial economy is also characterized by a greater demand for skilled labor and educated workers, which has led to a decline in the prospects for modestly educated and unskilled workers, who are disproportionately black and Latino (but who also include many whites). In fact, the growth of wage inequality across color lines reflects an underlying shift in the fortunes of skilled and unskilled workers since the late 1960s. Highly educated workers, especially those with a college education, have seen their wages rise. Disagreeing with scholars who attribute black poverty solely to white racism, Andrews maintains that the impoverished black condition in America is connected to capitalistic structures that have left behind an American underclass and points to greater class disparities that cut across racial lines in the twenty-first century.

However, the convergence of race and class does reveal a different experience of poverty among blacks within an American underclass. Andrews asserts that blacks "were so badly discriminated against by historic American racism that they were unprepared for the sea change in the American and world economy that has utterly transformed our lives over the past three decades." Because blacks have been historically oppressed by white supremacy, when such economic shifts occurred, "black people were completely unprepared for, and unable to take advantage of these shifts." Yet, Andrews maintains that "even if every racist white person in this country had a change of heart or moved abroad, most poor black people would be exactly where they are right now in the absence of major changes in government policy to address issues of poverty and economic inequality across color lines."[28] Because economic institutions and structures within a post-industrial political economy generate economic oppression for a black underclass, combating racial injustice alone will not lift poor blacks out of poverty. Instead, there must be a turn to economic structures and practices that vitiate the opportunities of many racial members within an American underclass.

Racial oppression is often articulated as the fundamental injustice that structures the poverty of blacks in America. For example, although womanist theologians and ethicists delineate the intersections among race, class, and gender defining the impoverished experiences of poor black women, they do not uncover the complexities of how race and class converge in defining the opportunities of black women locked within an American underclass. I appreciate Andrews's nuanced articulation of the complexities associated with how an American underclass affects poor blacks and their experiences of poverty. It is important to note, however, that the American underclass phenomenon and its problems of inequitable economic structures go beyond race, as this permanent class also affects poor whites and Hispanics, although blacks are disproportionately represented.

While Andrews discusses how capitalism and an American underclass are linked to black poverty in America, I am particularly concerned with the unique impoverished experiences of a black underclass, which are qualitatively different from those of the larger American underclass. The truly disadvantaged cannot be seen as part of a monolithic black community that continues to experience oppression that is solely racial. When racial oppression is seen as the primary injustice committed against blacks, it obscures how economic structures and class inequalities destroy the opportunities of a growing black underclass. Although there has been an emerging black middle class in the economic shifts of the last three decades, a parallel black underclass has also resulted.

The socioeconomic dislocation experienced among blacks must be seen as having complex sociological antecedents that range from demographic problems to issues of economic organization. Structural constraints have intensified black poverty and social isolation among black communities. For instance, Wilson discloses the emergence of a post-industrial economy and its impact on poor black urban communities. He posits that there were "substantial job losses in the very industries in which urban minorities had greatest access and substantial employment gains in higher-education-requisite industries that are beyond the reach of most minority workers. Inner-city blacks were poorly prepared for these trends."[29] One can infer that this is why black employment rates have not responded well to current economic recovery plans. The chronic unemployment of poor blacks is grounded in a long history of economic shifts and their effects, including social alienation and economic dislocation. These effects are still deeply felt. In the face of the structural causes and constraints for poor blacks, the cultural-deficiencies argument is inadequate to explain present levels of inequality.

Moreover, this history of economic change also discloses another key structural constraint for poor blacks: education. As the economy shifted in the 1970s, many higher-education jobs did not really require higher-education training. Industries were institutionalizing job requirements based on technology that people could learn or operate without formal education.[30] However, formal education was associated with such skills. Because the education usually offered by inner-city schools "prepares minority youth for the low-wage sector, minorities, including black youth, have been unprepared to enter a changing workforce."[31]

Due to the modern industrial economy's transition from a producer to a service economy in the 1970s, joblessness became a significant feature of poor black communities. Not possessing the educational qualifications for a service-oriented economy, high school dropouts and high-school graduates in urban areas were faced with a "dwindling supply of career jobs offering the real earning opportunities available to them in the 1960s and early 1970s."[32] For example, "New York lost 135,000 jobs in industries in which workers averaged less than 12 years of education and gained more than 300,000 jobs in industries in which workers had 13 or more years of education."[33] These black communities began experiencing deeper, inter-generational cycles of deprivation and poverty not because of deficiencies within black culture but due to an American post-industrial economy that gave little value to urban black labor, which led to the greater economic and social vulnerability of these communities. Marla F. Frederick writes about similar effects and outcomes that the shifting economy had on rural blacks, particularly rural black women.[34]

Another negative factor is that the manufacturing jobs that were still present in the 1970s (including the large plants) relocated from urban to suburban areas, precipitating the demise and/or exodus of smaller stores, banks, and other businesses from these areas. In addition, urban blacks' travels to suburban jobs proved to be problematic because "28 percent or fewer had access to an automobile." The heavy travel expenses involved in daily travel to the suburbs were daunting for urban blacks. For certain, owning a car creates expenses beyond the purchase price. Consequently, many "urban blacks ended up spending more getting to work in the suburbs than getting paid."[35]

The erosion of wages and benefits also forced many low-income work-ers in the inner city to move or remain on welfare. Hence, the Moynihan Report's discussion of welfare among black women as the result of a breakdown in families misses the key reason that urban black women tended to remain on welfare: the political economy that locked them out of educational advancement and, therefore, employment opportunities with real earnings.

This structural lack of opportunity and advancement has had profound ramifications on the social behavior of vulnerable black communities that found themselves economically and socially marginalized. In impoverished urban areas such social behavior is especially visible in the actions of youth and young adults. Wilson writes that some young people grow up in a jobless environment that lacks the idea of work as a central experience of adult life, which means that they have little or no attachment to the labor force. These circumstances increase the likelihood that some of these young people will rely on illegitimate sources of income. In public policy debates on welfare reform and crime, discussions of behavior and social responsibil-ity fail to mention the structural underpinnings of poverty and welfare. The popular argument is that the individual must change, not the structures of society. Yet the disappearance of work from poor black communities points to the structural nature of black poverty.

In summary, American economic structures have exacerbated the inter-generational poverty among poor blacks, especially among black women. Such economic factors that have intensified deprivation in black communities challenge the neo-liberal narrative that black poverty is due to cultural deficiencies and personal irresponsibility or that poor black women are poor because they are indolent and lazy, leeching on the welfare system. Because black poverty is a structural problem largely intensified by the shift in American political economy, economic restructuring, not merely personal improvement, is essential to improving the material realities of these communities.

FALLING THROUGH THE CRACKS

Demographically, black poor people are distinguished from poor whites by certain social characteristics: "they are largely more female, younger, and usually reside in the urban ghetto."[36] Furthermore, at all ages, black women are much more likely to be poor than white females, white males, or black males.[37] For example, black women not only suffer from structural constraints on employment opportunities but also are often the sole caretakers of America's most impoverished group: black children. As a result, poverty among black women must be distinguished and described differently from poverty among other poor groups. Black women's poverty can be distinguished from black men's poverty in two respects. First, black women's experiences of inequities and inequalities are due to structural constraints in employment that keep them in traditionally female jobs as well as their experiences of poverty due to their unpaid domestic labor. Second, the impoverishment of black women is deeply connected to the poverty of black children.

Limited Opportunities for Women

Poor black women continue to experience inequity in employment and work. Sociologist Patricia Hill Collins notes that while "US black women are poor for many of the same reasons that US black men are poor—both lack access to steady, well-paying jobs that ensure an adequate income. . . . African-American women's confinement to a small segment of low-paying jobs reveals how race and gender converge."[38] Political scientist Julianne Malveaux notes that women who escape traditionally female jobs enjoy higher wages. However, black women have had less success than white women in moving out of traditionally female jobs. She states, "Although the quality of work among black women changed, it changed because black women moved from one set of stratified jobs to another, not because they left 'typically' female jobs."[39] Although black women, like black men, continue to experience a lack of steady access to well-paying jobs, black women continue to experience some of the lowest paying jobs.

African American women remain in typically "female" jobs such as file clerks, typists, social welfare clerical assistants, nurse aides, and homecare providers. Monica Jackson stated in 1990 that "African American women remain one of the lowest paid race and gender groups, making only $301 per week during 1989 compared to $334 for their white counterparts and $348 and $482 for African American and white men, respectively."[40] As of April 2008, "US women still earned only 77 cents on the male dollar. . . . (That number drops to 68% for African-American women and 58% for Latinas.)"[41]

Although black women have fared better than black men in the professional arena, a majority of black women in the poor working class and underclass receive the lowest wages, exacerbating the poverty they endure. Moreover, because unmarried women head over 50 percent of black families, any programs or policies for change and development of black communities must focus on the labor-market realities of these women.[42] Such labor market realities illuminate the unique ways that class, gender, and race converge to affect the opportunities of these women.

Poor black women's work is also deeply affected by the demographic shifts that have occurred in the inner city since 1970, shifts marked by a decrease in the median age of single, black mothers. By the early 1970s, unwed black teenage mothers populated over half of single-parent homes in the inner cities. Into 2011, 72 percent of black babies were born to unmarried mothers. Black teenage mothers tend to experience longer durations of poverty due to the disruption of their schooling, which contributes to their underemployment or unemployment. In fact, in inner cities "almost 40 percent of all births are to [unmarried] women under age twenty."[43] Adolescent mothers are the most disadvantaged of all female family heads because in addition to having their schooling interrupted, they very rarely receive child support. Thus, age is another constraint, and young black mothers rarely find opportunities to improve their situation. This demographic correlation between poverty and age remains important to understanding poor black women's unique experiences of deprivation.

In addition to low wages within typically female jobs and problems of age related to work, higher rates of poverty among black women are also due to their need to carry out unpaid domestic labor. African American women perform duties such as cooking, cleaning, childrearing, and other domestic labor without pay. Moreover, despite the fact that caring for a child is often seen as something that women "naturally" do better than men, childcare also constitutes unpaid labor. A considerable portion of black women's time goes into caring for their own children and those of others.[44] The problem of the public-private dichotomy in relation to "labor" adversely affects their income opportunities. Although poor black women's labor remains unpaid, "they do much of the shopping for housing, food, clothing, health care, transportation, recreation, and other consumer goods."[45] Because of these women's depressed incomes and consumer racism, poor black women do not have the purchasing power needed to survive and flourish. Although impoverished black women are castigated for being on welfare and not working, they complete much domestic labor without compensation.[46]

In the end, poor black women within a black underclass experience race/gender hierarchies that make their experiences of work, family, and poverty *different* and, at times, chronic. Nonetheless, despite their hardships, poor black women have historically demonstrated their resilience within the US political economy.

Historically, black women have participated in the labor force at much higher rates than their white counterparts, despite systemic discrimination, unemployment, and general lack of opportunity. Even with the high rates of unemployment among black women in the 1970s and 1980s, black women continued to display a solid commitment to the labor force. Some studies found that white women faced with unemployment are more likely than men to withdraw from the labor force, but patterns for black women keep pace with white men. Even in the current context of economic recession, black women continue to seek employment in spite of initial failures to find employment. When faced with prolonged joblessness, black women continue to seek employment at about the same rate as the total group of unemployed workers, which is predominantly male. Even though unemployment has remained high for blacks since the 2008 recession (double the national average, at 16.2 percent as of 2011), "more than half (54.3 percent) of employed blacks are women."[47] Black women continue to demonstrate their resilience and agency.

Black women's increased poverty as a group is not due to a culture of indolence and unwillingness to work but rather to structural constraints that no longer need their unskilled labor and have failed to prepare them for skilled labor. Statistics show that they persist in trying to find employment, asserting their agency in spite of systemic oppression and exploitation.

The Poverty of Black Children

As noted above, poverty among black women is also qualitatively different because of their role as caretakers to poor black children. Because single-parent female households raise a great percentage of black children, black children are affected by the same economic and social constraints as poor black women. Like impoverished black women, the forces that exclude and alienate poor black children from meaningful participation in American economic and social life have had adverse effects on their sense of growth and flourishing. These exclusionary forces include the shift in the economy as well as economic and social alienation from mainstream America.

Black children are profoundly influenced by the socioeconomic conditions of impoverished black women. Today, black children in young female-headed households are the poorest in the nation. While a black child born in the United States has a "one in two chance of being born poor, a black child in a female-headed household has a two in three chance of being poor. If that household is headed by a mother under twenty-five years of age, that baby has a four in five chance of being poor."[48] As the founder and president of the Children's Defense Fund, Marian Wright Edelman notes that we "often overlook the increasing importance of the parent's age in determining the family's income."[49] Edelman further notes that "the poverty rate among all families with heads under twenty-five was 29.4 percent in 1987, which was almost three times the national average at that time." Although the proportion of black women under the age of twenty giving birth has declined since the early 1970s, "the percentage of those births to unmarried teens since 1970 soared 50 percent."[50] Because black female teens are often undereducated or uneducated, their economic prospects are bleak, which structures the constraints and possibilities of their children.

As of 2011, the Children's Defense Fund found that the majority of America's black community, seven in ten adults, view these as "tough or very bad times" for black children, and many see poor black youth falling further behind. "Forty percent of black children are born poor, 85 percent of black children cannot read or do math at grade level in fourth grade, and almost half drop out of school." Moreover, a black boy born in 2001 has a "one in three chance of going to prison sometime in his lifetime."[51]

Parents' class standings have profound implications for their children's opportunities. Social inequalities among children are directly linked to the educational level, occupational status, income, and opportunities of their parents. Because poor black women and their children are denied the educational opportunities that are essential in a post-industrial political economy that links employment opportunities to increased educational attainment, they face intergenerational cycles of deprivation and poverty, contributing to profound limitations on future opportunities.

The Importance of Education

Sociologist Annette Lareau offers an example of how poverty affects black children within the educational system. The Lower Richmond School in the inner city of Richmond, Virginia, serves black students from kindergarten through fifth grade. To begin with, the school looks grim and unwelcoming. The building is "three stories tall and is surrounded by a high, gray chain linked fence." She describes the building as "old, with a dirty beige exterior and few windows" as well as "patches of paint blotched on the walls" to cover up regular graffiti. "There is an asphalt playground with some trees and patches of grass." Lareau remarks that Lower Richmond School's physical landscape is more "inviting" than other inner-city schools in the Richmond area where "beer bottles and broken glass litter the school yard."[52]

Although the Lower Richmond School is one of the more accomplished schools in the inner city, "about one-half of each class reads below grade level and about one-third of the fourth-grade cohort is about two years below grade level."[53] Lareau notes that "the district is under pressure to raise test scores, but the budget is very limited, and shortfalls occur annually."[54] Only a few parents attend or participate in the Parent-Teacher Association. Despite these grim statistics, the Lower Richmond School continues to be well regarded by parents and educators. In fact, one fourth-grade teacher, Ms. Berstein, "referred to Lower Richmond as a 'cream puff' compared to other inner-city schools."[55]

This description of the inner-city school of Lower Richmond attended by poor black children can be understood more clearly when contrasted with the many suburban schools in Richmond. In a suburb of Richmond, Lareau reports that the Swan School is a

> sprawling facility that consists exclusively of one-story buildings that are spread out over the school grounds. The buildings also have windows lining one entire wall of each classroom. Outside is an expanse of grass, where unlike Lower Richmond, Swan's school playground has an elaborate swing set and bars, with a red-hued mulch of shredded wood under the bars to protect children if they fall. Swan has no fence and the school looks open and inviting. In addition, it is located in a quiet, residential neighborhood where middle-class families live.[56]

At Swan, most children in fourth grade, including underachievers, perform at grade level. In reading, many students at Swan are two years above grade level, disclosing the quality of instruction as well as teacher-parent collaboration. Unlike Lower Richmond, Lareau states that "most children come from families where both parents are employed outside the home, often as professionals, such as lawyers, social workers, accountants, managers, teachers, and insurance executives."[57] Parents keep a close eye on teachers and do not hesitate to intervene and ask questions about their children's progress.

This comparative look at Swan and Lower Richmond demonstrates how the social class and standing of the parent(s) directly affect the opportunities of children within the educational system. Black children (as seen in Lower Richmond) suffer from a poor quality of education, education that is desperately needed for future opportunities. This lack of quality education is again due to structural inequalities: inner-city schools continue to be more underfunded, ill-equipped, and poorly staffed than suburban schools. Moreover, the poor quality education that poor black children experience is directly connected to the structural constraints imposed upon their parents, who are often poor, black, single, young mothers.

The economic and social alienation experienced by impoverished black women and children has greatly contributed to the educational and social challenges that face black children and youth. Poor black children experience painful feelings of humiliation, frustration, and anger from the poverty and job loss experienced by their families due to the shifts in the US economy. As a result, these children often protest against the socioeconomic forces that continue to exclude them. While destructive and counterproductive, I have heard kids talk about shoplifting, for example, as a way of overcoming the barriers of inflated prices. Black youth express their existential pain in response to the alienating forces of post-industrialism when they play loud music to establish their presence in streets and parks or spray paint their graffiti signatures on the walls of buildings. Their derogation of white police officers "reflects long traditions of resistance to the most visible agents of racism and social control in their neighborhoods."[58] While this aggressive behavior is detrimental to their well-being and flourishing, such behavior is part of an infra-politics of the poor directed at resisting the forces that constrain them. Historian Carl Nightingale argues that "the phenomenal artistry of the folklore of the urban toasts, the language of the hustler, and all of hip-hop culture have helped immeasurably to articulate inner-city young people's searches for self-worth."[59]

In the end, poor black children are the recipients of the poverty and helplessness that are features of the reality of many poor black women. They have a need to resist and subvert such hopelessness, thus undermining the shame, humiliation, and despair that accompany intergenerational poverty.

Inequalities within the American political economy reveal both the despair and resilience that poor black women and children often experience. When reflecting on how the economic resources of a black underclass are systematically exploited, one must acknowledge that the logic of free-market ideology and meritocracy obscures the real experiences of poor black women. As Marcellus Andrews rightly assesses, "The problem poor blacks now face is that a terrible new synthesis of racism, free markets, and meritocracy has replaced the old system of organized Negrophobia that has been our nemesis for three hundred years."[60] If the opportunities of poor black women are to improve, we must challenge the gross inequities of the American political economy in order to address the adverse experiences of poverty that black women confront.

When reviewing the actual economic miseries of black women in an American underclass, it is clear that black churches must be informed by the social sciences about how to cultivate political wisdom in dealing with the contemporary problem of black women's poverty; they must be familiar with the destructive assumptions employed by approaches such as those of charitable choice. Poor black women are also a part of America. Their experiences of economic suffering must be acknowledged and embraced if black churches and other black religious institutions are to create spaces in which black women can experience hope and flourish, regardless of their economic status.

If black churches are to participate effectively in projects of hope and renewal for poor black women, they will serve themselves well by a much greater knowledge of the findings and implications of social-science research in relation to black women's poverty in the twenty-first century. This is a serious task, and in fact, there is no other way to develop accurate knowledge about how historical shifts in American political economy have intensified and exacerbated poverty, engendering a black underclass within a larger American underclass. While race and gender are important in analyzing black women's poverty, grasping the nature of the economic inequities poor black women endure within American political economy is highly significant. Black churches must fully engage the reality of multiple black Americas. Class does matter.

4

Guilty until Proven Innocent

As economic structures in America change, so public policies also change. Public policies continue to exacerbate economic inequities and cultural inequalities for poor black women. On August 22, 1996, President Clinton signed into law the Personal Responsibility and Work Opportunity Act (PRWORA), which championed distorted cultural perceptions of poor black women in relation to social welfare in America. What was striking about the signing process was the presence of two black women standing alongside the president. These two black women, encircled by a group of white men, were portrayed as "having come to their senses" about responsibility and work, disavowing their previous laziness and dependency for a newfound attitude of hard work for personal success. This portrayal fed into the stereotypical images and representations of poor black women discussed earlier in the book. For certain, some people were left with a perplexing feeling as to why these two black women represented a poor population that is primarily white. Why was it necessary to use these stereotypical images of welfare recipients to justify PRWORA, which was the policy foundation for the legislation TANF (Temporary Assistance for Needy Families)? What message was being sent to the American public?

It is interesting to note that these stereotypical images of poor black women within public policies are supported and sustained by larger religious values within black communities and the broader American culture. Protestant religious values that demonize poverty as ultimately an individual's failure (failure as an unwillingness to take advantage of God's or Creation's "abundance") continue to reinforce and solidify neo-liberal rhetoric. This religious viewpoint is certainly expressed in some black churches, which causes these institutions to work against the very people they purport to help. Black churches must fully engage this reality.

Such Protestant religious values must be deconstructed and challenged because these values do not acknowledge how economic inequalities such as the absence of a living wage, healthcare, and childcare are governed and sustained by unjust public policies, in particular, policies that regulate and control adversely the material realities of poor black women. They are often guilty until proven innocent by policies that stigmatize them. One such particular public policy that negatively affects poor black women is welfare reform.

While welfare in general has been a boon to poor black women to assist in caring for themselves and their children, it has equally been a bane due to the social stigmatization and inequitable economic practices associated with it. Specifically, welfare discourse is fatally flawed because it often characterizes welfare recipients as immoral women, primarily *black*, who are irresponsible and neglectful of their tasks as mothers and contributors to society. This perception of welfare women as irresponsible and lazy *black* women has its origins in racist modes of discourse that have unjustly equated black women with welfare mothers or "queens," disregarding the fact that most women who receive welfare continue to be white women. Such biased neo-liberal logic that guides policy decisions often involves the assumption that poor black women are morally culpable for their impoverishment.

In this chapter I argue that Protestant religious values often influence and shape US public policies, especially those connected with social services that regulate and control poor black women's lives. In particular, religious communities, including black churches, must acknowledge and challenge how racist, conservative values have shaped the history of welfare policy in America and the structural violence that causes for the poor. Policy is not unrelated to religious values in American life. Instead, policy feeds upon and draws its ideological legitimation from the Protestant religious values that many black churches embrace. This chapter critically analyzes the ways in which religious values adversely influence welfare reform. Moreover, it explores how welfare collaborates with what can be called the New Jane Crow, a legalized but racist system that is creating a new caste structure among women of color (particularly poor black women) through the prison industrial complex. Welfare policy has become a form of structural violence in that it continues to control and regulate in a negative way participation in the labor force, reproductive capacities, and the cultural capital of poor black women.

AN UNHOLY ALLIANCE:
RELIGIOUS VALUES AND NEO-LIBERAL LOGIC
IN WELFARE REFORM

Public policymaking is social, political, and economic, but also deeply religious. Public policies are often grounded in religious moral sensibilities concerning the nature of people and institutions, even though this is often unconscious and unacknowledged. From this country's beginning, moral concepts and practices have fueled public policy decisions.

Such religious viewpoints in public policy debates are often left unexamined. For example, under the guidance of the George W. Bush administration, charitable choice grew out of conservative Protestant evangelical values. Faith-based initiatives reflect a religious tradition "that focuses on the individual and a nineteenth-century philanthropic tradition in which the wealthy not only distributed handouts, they also imposed demands and discipline on the poor."[1] The conservative Protestant values that undergirded charitable choice are best expressed in Marvin Olasky's book *The Tragedy of American Compassion,* in which Olasky makes his argument for compassionate conservatism. Compassionate conservatism is a concept that supports the dismantling of the welfare state in favor of charitable works, funded through federal grants and partnerships between church and state. Olasky maintains that the government should empower local private charities to provide for those who are poor and vulnerable.[2]

Another book, *America's Providential History* by Mark Beliles and Stephen McDowell, was used in the 2004 Republican Party platform to suggest that the biblical "dominion mandate" supported and reflected Bush's economic, social, and environmental programs.[3] Based on an interpretation of Genesis 1:26, the "dominion mandate" calls on Christian persons to "rule over" all of creation, which includes the control of government institutions. For Beliles and McDowell, scripture mandates a "godly" rule within society in which "the godly" are responsible for overseeing all aspects of life. Indeed, the book offers a biblical rationale for many of the policies of the Bush administration. Among other topics, the book provides a theological justification for supporting state and federal tax cuts. Beliles and McDowell view taxes as unbiblical; income tax is "idolatry," property tax is "theft," and inheritance taxes are simply not allowed in the Bible.[4] In their interpretation, scripture makes it clear that God is the provider, not the state, and that impoverished individuals are to be cared for by private acts of charity.

These authors also describe the Christian responsibility as fundamentally concerned with increasing wealth in our society. They state: "A secular society will lack faith in God's providence and consequently men will find fewer natural resources."[5] They further posit that the Christian knows that God's potential is unlimited and that there is no shortage of resources in God's earth. Such rhetoric communicates an ideology of abundance in which the poor are interpreted as persons who lack faith or simply do not participate in the abundance that God offers. In addition to being radically non-inclusive and imperial, this ideology ignores the inequitable arrangements and power relations that cause and perpetuate deprivation and poverty within any society. Moreover, this ideology sponsors religious values that inform policy decisions adverse to the well-being of the poor, including black women.

A basic religious tenet within this ideological conservatism is that success is connected to people doing God's will. For Protestant conservatism, one's financial success is directly related to the blessings God gives for living a life of obedience to one's vocation and call, which includes being faithful to hard work. If financial health is the reward for one's faithfulness in working hard, then poverty is a direct result of an absence of hard work, an unwillingness to fulfill one's vocation. From this perspective, poverty is the result of vice and the failure to do the will of God. Unfortunately, this religious worldview does not take into account the structural realities and lived experiences of those who are impoverished in the United States.

Another policy initiative sponsored by evangelical Protestant religious values was the Healthy Marriage Initiative proposed by the Bush administration in 2004, which provided economic incentives to women who stayed married before or after childbirth. A central religious assumption of this initiative was that marriage would solve the problem of poverty among black women. It assumed that the social and economic problems black women confront are due to their single status. Interestingly, the government website for this initiative argued that "poor black women who attended church were 73 percent more likely to marry than non-church-going black women," which framed these women's socioeconomic issues as fundamentally a religious and moral problem.[6]

Religion is often seen as integral in defining (and policing) the parameters of black women's moral and sexual relations. However, this approach ignores a fundamental fact. Marriage has not historically been the route out of poverty for black women that it has been for white women. Bush's marriage initiative assumes that families headed by single black women are poor because these women are unmarried. However, the relationship between poverty and single motherhood is much more complex. Single black mothers are not more likely to be poor because they are not married. They are likely not to be married because they (and likely their potential marriage partners) have poor economic prospects. For many black women and black men, a good job may be a prerequisite for marriage.

Clearly, the Healthy Marriage Initiative reflects a neo-liberal reading of black women's poverty indicating that their deprivation is singularly based on their own wrongdoings and mishaps. In no way does this policy show how it could lead to a just distribution of resources and power, which is most needed in combating impoverishment not only among black women but also among poor persons in any community. Nor does this initiative consider the high rates of domestic violence that poor black women endure, which complicates the "marriage is the answer" mantra. Instead of attending to structural injustices, this initiative attempts to police the sexuality and personal lives of poor black women. In fact, Bush's initiative continued to reinforce their deprivation and poverty. Unfortunately, this kind of thinking continues to dominate discourses on poor black women.

Using religious viewpoints to reinforce the idea that an individual is both the cause of and the solution to poverty deflects attention from the social and economic systems that perpetuate and exacerbate inequalities (while touting that the United States is a country that allows all to flourish and thrive). These religious views and their alliance with neo-liberal logic function to mask the fact that the majority of the poor are locked inside an American underclass, ensuring intergenerational cycles of structural inopportunity and inequality. Moreover, these religious viewpoints enable political leaders to place wealth and profit at the center of all major public policy decisions.

We need public policies that are more complex than those that "focus on the conversion of individual souls."[7] Similar to charitable-choice policies, welfare reform policies were also designed with an eye toward improving the individual morality of poor individuals to the exclusion of examining how our entire socioeconomic structure creates, sustains, and reproduces chronic deprivation. While some religious values emphasize personal or private moral norms, other religious values are under-emphasized, such as public morality, social justice, equitable working conditions, corporate responsibility, and so forth. This is a problem. Poverty in the United States is, in large part, systemic: inadequate political and economic policies produce systems that deprive people of jobs, living wages, access to healthcare, adequate housing, and quality education.

Nonetheless, such systemic oppression does affect individuals within poor communities, often leading to a sense of despair, hopelessness, and fear—the breeding ground for survival by any means necessary. Hence, creating public policies grounded in a religious view and the neo-liberal assumption that people are poor because they are failures does not honestly portray the experiences of impoverished communities across America.

What I have termed an unholy alliance between destructive religious values and neo-liberalism is especially seen in negative descriptions of poor black women on welfare. They are the "face" of welfare and poverty in America and, consequently, in need of moral reform. Such religious views and neo-liberal rhetoric do not take into account the actual experiences of black women in relation to poverty and welfare.

THE "RACIALIZING" OF WELFARE POLICY: A SILENCED HISTORY

The racializing of welfare is a persistent and unfortunate experience that poor black women endure. In a variety of contexts single black mothers who are welfare recipients are "viewed as a moral contagion destroying the ethical fabric of society."[8] Public discourse often bears witness to the assumption that welfare recipients are largely African American women who are too lazy to work for a wage, capitalizing on taxpayers' dollars instead of assuming responsibility for their livelihoods and futures. Images of black welfare mothers who enjoy taking advantage of the system continue to pervade the media and public discourse on welfare, which in turn exacerbates prejudice toward the very black women who genuinely need economic help. These stereotypical images of black women "blacken" the face of welfare to the extent that welfare is often perceived as a black woman's problem and a program that is in desperate need of overhaul.

Mythical images of black women continue to shape the ideas of welfare policy. Ethicist Traci West delineates the images that have been disseminated in the media:

> For instance, a degrading caricature of a black woman . . . grabbing for cash appeared on the editorial page of the *Globe*. . . . The most prominent silhouette in the center of the illustration was a female with an Afro hairstyle, a wide nose, and baby on her hip, who was also reaching up to get some cash.[9]

These images of black welfare mothers perpetuate a message that allows the public to believe that impoverished black women are greedy, cash-hungry, and manipulative recipients who "pimp" the system. These women are portrayed as using welfare benefits to increase their wealth and the wealth of their offspring. In addition, these women are illustrated as *morally* depraved for exploiting the welfare system in this way. Such gross objectification of black women enables welfare discourse to demonize black women as a moral contagion, central to the many problems of welfare policy.

Furthermore, black women are viewed as refusing to work and even "using their procreative abilities to secure more money."[10] An image of a black woman who already has four children and is pregnant again is used to communicate black women's proclivities toward moral destitution and greed. Poor black women are also seen as "black matriarchs," the "domineering female heads of the black family" in the United States.[11] The black matriarch "opens the floodgates for social theorizing about the intergenerational character of black poverty through the transmission of poor family values within black families."[12] This particular image interprets black women as emasculating and displacing black men, which is seen as leading to the disintegration of black families.

In addition, the "blackening" of welfare policy discourse presents the image of a black woman as the "typical" welfare recipient. It names black women as morally inferior and in need of moral and ethical reform in order to be contributing members of society "like their white counterparts." This racializing of welfare denounces black women as unworthy of public assistance.

Sociologist Mimi Abramovitz notes that this racializing of welfare policy discourse has historical roots. At its inception in 1935, the welfare state in America provided an infrastructure intended to "maintain families, the labor force, and the general welfare of society through the redistribution of working people's income to those who were not employed."[13] Such programs were efforts to modify market forces in order to provide security and stability for those whose income was interrupted by disability, widowhood, illness, or unemployment. One of these programs included the Social Security Act. This program was described as "dignified entitlement" because no proof of entitlement or "means test" was required to secure income support, since recipients were automatically entitled to these benefits by virtue of their participation in the labor force.[14] As briefly discussed in Chapter 2, social security recipients benefited from the welfare state that developed in the wake of the Great Depression after World War II. This historical approach to understanding the origin of the welfare state is important because today the welfare state is often understood only in terms of welfare for poor women of color.

Another program that was implemented was Aid to Dependent Children (ADC). This program was described as "humiliating relief" because recipients had to prove that they were qualified to receive income support. Proof of eligibility was particularly humiliating for single mothers, as they were subjected to degrading investigations concerning their private lives in order to verify their status. Initially, ADC was offered only to assist children who "lacked parental support as a result of death, long-term absence, or the incapacity of family."[15] As a result, it was available only to the children of primarily white widows or children whose parents were estranged or incapacitated. This excluded black women in record numbers during the twentieth century.

In 1962, ADC was revised into AFDC (Aid to Families with Dependent Children), expanding welfare access to black women as well. Abramovitz notes that the expansion of ADC was due, in large part, to grassroots organizing and the Civil Rights movement; it "provided some respite from the previously rigid eligibility rules, altering welfare's historic unresponsiveness to black women."[16] These shifts toward welfare's expansion were also in response to the rapid rise in the number of black families headed by females. It was also "influenced by the participation of black women in the Welfare Rights Movement, which encouraged them to lobby for their right to income support."[17] AFDC created new provisions that allowed women to work while receiving benefits. Because black women's participation in America's labor force has never been optional, these new provisions gave black women (en masse) access to welfare for the first time.

Nonetheless, there remained a need to identify deserving single mothers, and it is not surprising that the "undeserving" mothers were usually poor, black, and single. Welfare policy had to develop new criteria that reinforced the concept of the "worthy mother as the white mother."[18] Because black women have historically been described as morally and ontologically inferior to white women, black mothers continued to be vilified and labeled as unworthy welfare recipients. These welfare policies continued to objectify black womanhood as the dark shadow of white womanhood.

Such distinctions between white and black women receiving welfare benefits have deeper implications about the types of claims such women are able to make in relation to the state. Historian Michael Katz rightly notes that historical relief for the poor (private and public assistance) "has reflected and reinforced an enduring set of moral distinctions, divisions, and classifications among the poor."[19] These moral and social distinctions, often gendered and racialized, determine the "appropriate basis for claiming social rights such as need, financial contribution, and citizenship."[20] These distinctions also influence the ways in which recipients are engaged and treated. Poor black women continue to endure such social distinctions that name them as the "face" of welfare, which also renders white female welfare recipients altogether invisible in welfare discourse.

Although this demonizing of black women has historical roots going back to slavery, current stigmatizing of these women continues to bar these women from being seen by society as genuine mothers in need of real economic help and relief. Moreover, this racializing of welfare policy discussions and practices has the end result of maintaining capitalist privilege. These stigmatizing images are often internalized by black women, becoming images that inhibit their sense of self-actualization. Indeed, poor black women are profoundly affected by the racializing of welfare discourse and policy.

The contemporary racializing of welfare policy is also rooted in Ronald Reagan's administration and its War on Welfare programs. One of Reagan's goals was to dismantle the welfare state, which he interpreted as one of the major causes of the nation's economic woes during the 1980s. For the Reagan administration, personal responsibility and self-sufficiency were the answers to poverty. This perspective of personal responsibility and self-sufficiency

> precluded the President from understanding not only the problems faced by victims of systemic oppression—members of various racial

and ethnic minority groups confined to ghettos and women—many of whom were jobless through no fault of their own, but the plight of millions of others as well, including white men and women who were working but who could not support themselves and their families on their meager earnings.[21]

From 1980 to 1981, for example, there were "approximately eleven million welfare recipients, seven million of whom were children." Of the four million adults who received assistance, "most were mothers who were working for inadequate wages or who had been working and were unemployed but were looking for other jobs."[22] Studies show that the overwhelming majority of these women remained on welfare for shorter periods of time, usually to cope with temporary unemployment or some other crisis. These studies also showed that they preferred work to public assistance, if their work could keep them above poverty level to care for their children.[23] Contrary to the Reagan administration's assumption, these women were not personally irresponsible or women who refused to work. These women desired to work insofar as their basic needs could be met. As noted earlier, black women have demonstrated a remarkable resilience and participation in the US labor market over the last few decades.

However, for Reagan, the key to solving the welfare problem was cutting back on assistance and removing federal programs that aided the needy. Despite multiple studies there was a persisting belief that such women simply opted for dependency. Consequently, it was argued that the key to solving the welfare problem involved returning social responsibility for the poor to local communities (churches, private foundations, businesses, and charitable organizations). It was argued that welfare assistance should not be the responsibility of hardworking taxpayers. Yet, recent studies and public disclosures reveal that there is more fraud and abuse in the nation's tax system, its defense industry, or in the healthcare professions, and private charities than in the public welfare system—fraud and abuse that are far more costly to American taxpayers.[24]

Even though welfare is not the primary cause of national deficits and has helped poor women across racial categories survive day-to-day economic hardships, welfare has also been a bane for poor black women. The racialization of welfare with its deep roots in the mythical black woman who is overly sexual, indolent, and dependent on the system criminalizes them. This racialization of poverty is deeply influenced by the ways in which public discourse has shaped welfare policy to the extent that such women have often been blamed for the economic chaos of American society. This approach blames the victims of systemic oppression rather than acknowledging the inequitable structures that perpetuate and exacerbate cycles of poverty for poor black women and other communities. Perspectives of poor black women as "undeserving" welfare recipients have adversely affected the fashioning of welfare policy. As a result, welfare policy has led, in many ways, to the regulation of black women's lives and bodies.

THE REGULATION OF POOR BLACK WOMEN'S LIVES: THE NEW JANE CROW

Welfare policy continues adversely to regulate and control the material realities of poor black women in America in a multitude of ways. As noted before, public assistance for women emerged out of an array of social welfare programs such as Medicare and Social Security. While the broader welfare state has provided a safety net for the elderly and poor, it has also attempted to regulate various aspects of poor women's social lives, particularly poor black women who are generally understood as undeserving. Through its collaboration with the prison industrial complex, welfare policy tends to regulate three fundamental aspects of life among black women: their participation in the labor market, their reproductive capacities, and their cultural capital.

Imprisonment of Blacks

In 2010, African American legal theorist Michelle Alexander's *The New Jim Crow* incited a national conversation on the relationship among race, poverty, and incarceration. In this book, Alexander argues that a caste system based on race has reemerged in America. Beginning with the War on Drugs of the Reagan administration, poor black men within urban areas were deliberately targeted as the government decided to "get tough on" drugs and crime. Poor black men in inner cities were given extremely harsh prison sentences for selling crack cocaine, although many sociological scholars have documented that white middle-class men not only used powder cocaine at equal or greater rates than black men used crack cocaine but also did not receive commensurate prison sentences. Because these black men were primarily young, poor, and first-time offenders, they often did not have the type of legal counsel needed to protect them from certain plea bargains that labeled them felons for life.

Consequently, a large majority of African American men in some cities, like Chicago, for example, are named felons. These men are part of a growing caste (not underclass), which is a group of people who are permanently relegated, *by law*, to second-class status. They can be denied "the right to vote, automatically excluded from juries, and legally discriminated against in employment, housing, access to education, and public benefits—much as their grandparents and great-grandparents were during the Jim Crow era."[25] Racial injustice is thus legitimated and codified by our laws and the prison system.

Alexander views this caste status of poor black men as part of a larger prison industrial complex, a term used to attribute the rapid expansion of the US inmate population to the growing political influence of private prison companies and businesses that supply goods and services to government prison agencies. Coined by Angela Davis in 1997, the term *prison industrial complex* usually implies a network of institutional actors who are motivated by potential profit rather than solely by rehabilitating criminals or reducing crime rates. Thus, it is a desire for monetary gain that has led to the growth of the prison industry and the number of incarcerated individuals. Alexander insightfully observes that we are told of America's triumph over its ugly history of discrimination, exclusion, and racial caste. However, this is far from the truth. There is a New Jim Crow in town, and the prison industrial complex is its first cousin.

Black Women in Prison

While Alexander focuses primarily on black men within the prison industrial complex, *poor women of color are the fastest-growing group being disenfranchised by public policies that support this prison industrial complex.* While almost one million women are under the control of the criminal justice system, over half of the female prison population is black. Overall, black women are seven times more likely than white women to be incarcerated, and in fifteen states African American women are incarcerated at rates ten to thirty-five times higher than white women.[26] In New York, nearly nine out of ten female prisoners are black or Latina. Despite their small numbers in the population overall, Native Americans are nevertheless ten times more likely than whites to be imprisoned.[27]

Women in prison are among the most oppressed and vulnerable populations in the United States. They are typically young, poor (35 percent earned less than $500 per month), heads of households, with limited education (less than 45 percent completed high school), mothers of young children, and not infrequently, homeless (up to 40 percent in some urban areas).[28] In addition, about 50 percent of women in prison have serious, long-term substance abuse problems and are in poor health. These women often have a number of health issues, such as STDs, HIV, and reproductive health problems. They also tend to be victims of childhood abuse and domestic violence (57 percent of women prisoners were abused physically and/or sexually at least once in the past).[29]

Most of these women are taken into custody today for the same kinds of crimes for which women have always been arrested: nonviolent theft, forgery, and prostitution. Only a small percentage of women are arrested for violent crime, "with three-fourths of those arrested for simple assaults."[30] Fewer than one-third of women are incarcerated for violent crimes of any kind. However, when women are offenders in violent crime, victims report that *over half the women offenders were white and just over one-third were black*.[31] This report belies the cultural assumptions that poor black women are somehow more predisposed toward crime.

The New Jane Crow disenfranchises poor black women in a number of ways. Like black men, they are denied the right to vote, automatically excluded from juries, and legally discriminated against in employment, housing, access to education, and public benefits. However, for poor black women, welfare policy has played a central role in upholding and reinforcing such disenfranchisement. The 1996 welfare reform act imposed a lifetime welfare ban on women convicted of possessing or selling drugs. The historical legacy of welfare reform and the aforementioned War on Drugs under Reagan's administration have combined to produce deleterious consequences for many low-income women, with a disparate impact on African American women and Latinas.

While a number of states have modified or eliminated the ban, other states like Georgia, where the 67 percent recidivism rate is among the nation's highest, continue to maintain the ban.[32] Convicted African American female felons have difficulty getting jobs even in good economic times, and public assistance and food stamps are critical income supports during the transition from prison to community living, particularly when these women are trying to reclaim custody of their children. Consequently, poor black women, who are normally first-time offenders are locked in a permanent cycle of deprivation due to welfare laws and policies that ban them from the assistance they need to change their lives. While welfare policy attempts to regulate and control black women's lives, private prison industries grow wealthier on the backs of these same women, who are denied desperately needed benefits in order to become productive citizens. Such laws only exacerbate the impoverishment already experienced by poor black women.

Participation of Black Women in the Labor Force

Welfare policy continues to limit the participation of black women in the labor market. Welfare reform measures such as 1996 TANF increase black women's vulnerability to poverty. A woman drug offender is unable to secure employment, which motivates her to reenter an underground economy to survive. For other poor black women, welfare reform supplies only a meager income, giving them no way to better their lives through increased earnings. In 1996, TANF shifted from welfare (entitlement programs through cash payments) to "workfare," in which women were required to get off welfare rolls within a certain time frame while they worked. The goal was that these women, beginning to work while on welfare, would make a full transition to work within a five-to-seven-year time period. However, TANF includes jobs that relegate recipients to the lowest wage-earning jobs. These women also lack access to healthcare and childcare, which are essential to continue employment. Welfare policy has the effect of pushing poor black women into jobs that do not pay a living wage. Consequently, welfare policy has not necessarily been a "safety net" for such women; rather, it has eclipsed their ability to thrive and flourish by relegating them to underpaid jobs and further exacerbating the impoverishment of the very women these policies claim to help.

Control of Reproductive Capacities

There is a long history in this country of the ways in which poor black women's reproductive capacities have been controlled. Another regulatory component of welfare has been the use of sanctions to discourage black women from having children; this has grown from increasing concern about poor black women who give birth out of wedlock.[33] Legal scholar Dorothy Roberts argues that one goal of welfare has been to reduce the number of children born to women receiving public assistance; for example, the Family Law Cap is a birth-deterring provision. Roberts notes, "Under the family cap, a family's standard of need is not adjusted upward to accommodate the new child. These laws are premised on the assumption that the promise of benefits entices women to have additional children."[34]

Regulating reproduction through welfare has also included incentives based on birth control targeted at women within an underclass. One such medication is the FDA-approved Norplant, a synthetic hormone that suppresses ovulation and prevents pregnancy up to five years. Cultural anthropologist Dána-Ain Davis writes at length about the ways in which Norplant has been dispensed in inner-city communities that are primarily populated by poor black women.

> Politicians in . . . states such as Kansas, Connecticut, Louisiana, Arizona, Colorado, Ohio, Florida, and Washington have offered financial incentives to welfare recipients if they agree to use Norplant. The most coercive form of reproductive regulation through welfare with regard to Norplant were [*sic*] bills introduced in the states of Maryland, Mississippi, and South Carolina, which would have required that all recipients of welfare be mandated to get Norplant inserted as a condition of eligibility for welfare benefits.[35]

Davis discloses the coercive, regulatory function of welfare policy upon black women's bodies and reproductive choices through highlighting this

Norplant debacle. In addition, restrictions on black women's reproductive capacity have been legitimated by the argument that although black women make up only 6 percent of the US population, they represent one-third of welfare recipients. Such regulation of black women's bodies and reproductive choice raises questions about the "benign" nature of welfare policy.

Limitations on Cultural Capital

Welfare policy also regulates the cultural capital of poor black women. As discussed earlier, images of poor black women as "welfare queens" and "black matriarchs" by the media, politicians, and scholars strengthen misconceptions about black women and welfare. Black women are offered up as "the agent of destruction, the creator of the pathological Black urban poor family from which all ills flow; a monster creating crack dealers, addicts, muggers, and rapists—men who become those things because of being immersed in her culture of poverty."[36] Poor black women are seen as unworthy, undeserving users of welfare. They are considered to be opportunists of welfare and lazy matriarchs.

Because poor black women are vilified for their impoverishment and subsequent welfare use, they are hindered in building needed cultural capital such as respect and social dignity within larger social structures. Many politicians continue to blame welfare dependency on black women, arguing that black women are to blame for both broader society's social ills *and* high rates of taxation.[37] In fact, many conservatives and right-wing scholars suggest that "crime, unemployment, and single parenthood are caused by welfare as opposed to structural deficits."[38]

Political scientist Lawrence Mead, for example, contends that the welfare system "creates dependency because recipients are able to collect benefits without any responsibility to give back."[39] A neo-liberal assumption undergirding Mead's argument is that if programs like welfare (AFDC, TANF, and so on) did not exist, poor people would be forced to become "dependent on employment" rather than welfare, increasing the likelihood of two-parent families.[40] This argument assumes that welfare discourages black women from marriage and encourages them to have more children in order to increase their benefits. Such arguments do not allow poor black women to be seen as citizens contributing to society. Instead, poor black women are seen instead as contributing to social disorder.

In addition, some scholars unfairly blame poor black women for the sociologically constructed "depraved condition" of the black family. Black sociologist E. Franklin Frazier argues that black family and kinship ties were broken during slavery, contributing to the continuing instability of black families. In particular, he argues that poor black families have often resulted from matriarchal household structures. For him, the problem with black families is that black female heads of households have displaced male dominance. The currency of his claim continues to find residence in current welfare logic. There continues to be an assumption that the matriarchal familial structure leads to poverty, black boy criminals, and a host of other social ills. These distorted perspectives also impede poor black women's ability to build the cultural capital that could earn them respect within the larger society.

Degradation by Ritual

Poor black women's lives are also regulated by "welfare rituals of degradation." Black women welfare recipients are often subject to what Dána-Ain Davis refers to as "ceremonies of degradation" in the form of social services procedures and practices that are intended to humiliate and degrade. Davis describes this as a "dismantling of a woman's sense of self-worth and pride through procedures that dehumanize the public assistance encounter between social services worker and black female client." An example is the spatial arrangements of many social service offices, which appear to be set up to reinforce the "practice of social shaming."[41] Davis describes the social services office in "Lanville, New York"[42]:

On the floor, approximately two feet from the window, running its length, is a strip of worn red tape. The instructions read, "DO NOT CROSS THE LINE UNTIL YOU ARE CALLED." One is notified to approach the window only after a worker has nodded his or her head. You state your name and the purpose of your visit. The prescreeners fill out an orange card, stamp it using a punch-in clock, and instruct individuals to "sit down and we'll announce your name." When a name is called over the intercom, instructions are given to pick up one of three phones mounted on the walls. Each phone is a different color, which helps clients distinguish which one they are to pick up, so they can speak directly to a caseworker after being told to do so. As a result, conversations between recipients and caseworkers are easily overheard, and recipients, or potential recipients, often plead their cases to ensure receipt of assistance.

Because the window counters are so low, about crotch-level for someone 5'3", prescreeners rarely look at anyone standing in front of them. In fact, most of the time, frontline staff only talk to each other. It is quite humiliating to have a human being make little or no contact when you are [in] need.[43]

Another ritual of degradation involves local governments that use their welfare populations to meet campaign promises made to various business sectors, which often include promising to provide cheap labor to these companies. This has happened, according to Davis, in Lanville, New York, whose economic environment is characterized by downsizing, outsourcing, and contingent labor. Davis describes Leslie, one of the African American welfare recipients of Lanville, who was so embarrassed by her low salary that she could not discuss it with her friends:

> Directed by the welfare office, she went to work at a company that participated in New York's welfare-to-work program. However, the company barely paid her enough to cover her basic expenses, including care for her children. While Leslie said she wanted to return to school to get an associate's degree to secure a job that paid more, she was directed instead to a training program for a job that kept her in a perpetual cycle of deprivation. This was done with no consultation of Leslie's goals or ability to succeed, but on the needs of the private sector.[44]

Women involved in such programs are often enrolled in training programs that do not actually match their capabilities or self-identified goals. For example, Davis describes Sherita who had a good employment history and a strong sense of what she wanted to do with her life. She wanted to attend a school to study social work and believed she could attain her goal by taking classes at a local college. "No effort was made to help her secure employment in the area in which she already had expertise, nor was any effort made to support her educational goals. Instead, she attended a training school in which she had no interest simply to maintain eligibility for assistance."[45] When Davis asked the commissioner of social services in Lanville why Sherita was forced to take this line of work, the commissioner replied, "Look, if the person wants to be a hairdresser but the employment demand is for data-entry clerks, then that's the training we will give them."[46] In other words, these women are trained for jobs that align with what is driving the economy of Lanville.

Another degrading ritual involves regulating the childcare activity of poor black women who are welfare recipients. Historically, patriarchal ideology in the United States has promoted the idea that women should dedicate themselves to unpaid domestic work rather than wage-earning labor. Commitment to motherhood was viewed as a primary component of a healthy society. However, this perspective of mothering is often situated within a politics of race and class in which all mothers are not seen as entitled to such support. From the early 1900s to the early twentieth century, support was awarded only to white widowed mothers because they were considered the ideal for domestic labor. Consequently, poor black women did not qualify for these benefits and were forced into low-wage work in order to survive. They simply did not "fit" into the patriarchal ideology that supported the mothering of children. While I am not upholding such patriarchal ideology, I am attempting to disclose how the politics of mothering played out in the arena of race relations in America.

This "politics of mothering has been restaged based on these twentieth-century norms." Welfare policies actively penalize poor black women if they are not attached to work that is mandated (which tends to end up being jobs below the poverty-level line). In linking assistance to work in this way, welfare policy interferes with poor black women's mothering choices. It also "restricts their freedom between home and the market." This often presents an insurmountable obstacle for poor black women on welfare because "childcare stands in the forefront of anxiety about welfare reform because the mandate to work does not come with an assurance of a living wage."[47] When earnings are low, the level of childcare determines whether a woman's family will survive.

WELFARE POLICY AND STRUCTURAL VIOLENCE

Regulations produced by welfare policy for poor black women also intersect with high rates of domestic violence. The problem of domestic violence is perpetuated and exacerbated by welfare mandates that ignore the violent realities that women of color experience, particularly black women. These experiences of violence are reinforced by welfare reform measures that dismiss such experiences and the ways in which these experiences impede poor black women's capacity to fulfill the requirements demanded to receive welfare benefits. As a result, welfare policy itself becomes a form of structural violence; the policy supports structures that do not take into account factors that cannot be controlled but that do contribute to poor black women's deprivation.

Domestic Abuse

Connections among welfare, poverty, and violence frustrate many poor black women's efforts to thrive. Contemporary research suggests that "black women experience violence to a greater degree than other women, that they are more vulnerable to control by the state, and that they make up the largest percentage of women on welfare, but not the highest number." Black women's reported rates of intimate partner violence are 35 percent higher than the reported rates of white females. Moreover, black women "report intimate partner violence at a rate 22 percent higher than women of other ethnicities."[48] As a result, poor black women use welfare as an "immediate strategy to deal with domestic violence."[49]

For example, Davis refers to a thirty-eight-year-old African American woman named Clemmie, who accessed welfare to escape her abuser. Clemmie had four children who excelled in school. Clemmie's abuser became violent over time, even holding a gun to her head in front of a group of family and friends. Out of fear, many of her family members, including her sister and mother, alienated themselves from her and her situation. Davis remarks, "The more Clemmie tried to get out of the relationship, the more violent her abuser became. After her abuser threatened to kill her and her children for refusing to sell drugs, she fled, seeking refuge at a shelter for victims of domestic violence."[50] Clemmie's story contradicts the image of welfare women as lazy and indolent, capitalizing on the taxpayers' dollars. Her need for welfare was a direct result of the abuse she endured. She simply needed the means to establish a safe home for herself and her children.

It has been noted, however, that claims of domestic violence are not always believed by the welfare agencies. Davis recounts the story of an eighteen-year-old African American female named Leslie, who sought public assistance for herself and her unborn child in response to the domestic violence she experienced at the hands of her mother.

> Leslie stated to the caseworker in her first interview that she could not seek assistance from her mother because they "fought." The caseworker interpreted Leslie's statement to mean that she and her mother had "passionate arguments." When Leslie attempted to clarify what she meant, the caseworker became deeply suspicious. The caseworker was visibly annoyed and told Leslie that "she'd better think about what she had said because the charge of parental abuse is very serious." Leslie, deeply offended and hurt, got up from her seat and left the office. The caseworker embodied an adversarial role, mistreating Leslie based on her own stereotypical images of poor black women. Leslie, a victim of abuse, turned to welfare for a particular reason.[51]

Like many others, she was economically dependent on her abuser; she had few resources and no other means of support. Public assistance would have provided an opportunity for her to leave her abusive situation.[52]

Leslie's victimization was colored by race. As was true in this instance, some caseworker interactions and practices mirror broader societal tensions about black women on welfare, regardless of their status as victims of violence. A primary cause is that welfare reform policies often justify such prejudice about poor black women on welfare. They are thus viewed with disrespect and caution based on the imagined social destruction they cause or the fraud they commit. As a result, the line between poverty and criminality is often blurred. Welfare measures that reinforce erroneous ideological assumptions or conclusions about black women and welfare lead in turn to policies that exacerbate their poverty.

In addition, welfare-to-work requirements under the 1996 TANF welfare reform measure adversely affect poor black women who are victims of violence. Abusers often "maintain control over their victims by inflicting physical and psychological injuries, preventing many women from complying with the work requirements related to welfare."[53] Moreover, the inability to comply with such mandates means that these women lose their benefits and are likely to stay with or return to abusers because of their need for economic support.[54] Welfare-to-work requirements often ignore the real obstacles these women face as they attempt to move toward economic independence.

The Family Violence Option

The documented intersection between welfare and domestic violence has resulted in a protective measure for battered women: the Family Violence Option (FVO), which was an amendment to the 1996 PRWORA. FVO permits states, if they chose to implement it, "to screen welfare recipients for domestic violence, refer victims of domestic violence to counseling, and determine whether certain welfare requirements should be waived."[55]

However, there has been unequal access to FVO for poor black women on welfare. Historically, black women are rarely viewed as victims of violence, but instead, as women without virtue, which is one reason why various types of violence against black women are not addressed by the state.[56] Legal studies scholar Linda Ammons notes how ineffective the "battered woman syndrome" is as a defense in court for black women charged with murdering their abusers. Black women are simply not seen as victims,[57] and violence in the black community is viewed as normative.

Evelyn Barbee, a professor of health sciences, also notes that violence is often equated with the black community. She describes being attacked by a black man in a public venue; a passerby ignored her cry for help. She had an opportunity to ask the woman who heard and ignored her plea for help why she did nothing. The woman replied that she thought Barbee and the perpetrator were together.[58] For Barbee, this statement was characteristic of the way in which society sees violence within relationships as acceptable, especially within black communities.

In this country, at present, black women on welfare are often not credible as victims of violence. Little empathy is found for them within broader society. Crafting measures that provide protection for these women is essential. Black women who experience violence are bound by ideological constraints of unworthiness. Their ability to secure assistance, if they are on welfare, becomes more complex because their victim status is adversely affected by racial prejudices and stereotypes.

As long as the history of welfare and the way in which it sponsors structural violence for many black women are ignored, and religious values are unexamined, blaming poor black women for their deprivation will persist. This history must be deconstructed and challenged. Religious worldviews and values that buttress death-dealing public policies (such as welfare reform policy) for poor black women must be resisted and transformed when these policies collude with inequities within the American economy. Such policies that criminalize victims and collaborate with the New Jane Crow must be addressed and changed.

5

The Unfinished Business
of the
Poor People's Campaign

A New Gender and Sexual Politics

In light of the economic and policy miseries that poor black women endure, how might black churches strengthen their participation in a project
of hope and thriving for and with these women? The last four chapters
posit a major claim: poor black women experience economic inequities
that cut across racial groups and are subject to policies that make it difficult to flourish through their individual undertakings. In light of the economic and policy experiences of poor black women within an American
underclass, how might black religious institutions such as black churches
morally respond?

Because poor black women are part of a larger American underclass that
crosses racial affiliations, class-based responses are extremely important.
The Black Church does have moral resources to act courageously, creatively,
and imaginatively about prospects for the "least of these" within their own
communities. One such resource lies in resuscitating the vision and norms of
the Poor People's Campaign (PPC). Even though a cadre of black churches
historically conceptualized and galvanized participation in the PPC, the
work of this movement is largely unfinished business.

Initially conceived by Marian Wright Edelman and Martin Luther
King, Jr., in 1963, the PPC was a movement for economic justice that
articulated the necessity of promoting the flourishing and thriving of poor
persons across racial categories and divides. Five years later, on May 13,
1968, Resurrection City or the City of Hope in Washington, DC, was of-
ficially opened. Under the leadership of Ralph Abernathy and the Southern

Christian Leadership Conference (SCLC), Resurrection City was a semi-permanent camp set up near the Washington Monument in a spot where a couple of thousand poor persons resided as a protest against the economic injustices they faced in employment, healthcare, income, and education within America. The tent city was a symbolic reminder to the nation that its poor people had a vision of hope in a "just" society that should respond to the economic and material needs of all, especially its dispossessed and disinherited. The PPC sought to employ a class-based movement of the poor that was guided by the norms of inclusion and participation. However, Resurrection City quickly deteriorated, leaving the PPC as largely unfinished business.

This chapter contends that a critical retrieval of the PPC movement can help revive a class-based movement that works with and for the poor. Such a critical retrieval involves exploring the possibilities and limitations of the Black Church–led Poor People's Campaign. Led by a cadre of black church leaders, it has been described by some scholars as the last crusade of the Civil Rights movement. Dissimilar to the race-based protests to end legal segregation, the SCLC offered a class-based politics to address poverty in America across racial categories.

However, the SCLC and its anti-poverty campaign were not sensitive to the ways in which issues of gender and sexuality inform a class-based politics. Class-based politics that are not sensitive to gender and sexuality encourage a political economy of sexual dominance, which especially compromises poor black women. the SCLC's class-based politics involved sexist and heterosexist assumptions and constructions of black womanhood and manhood as well as black femininity and masculinity that affected the ideologies and practices employed by male leaders of the PPC and that also effectively excluded women from leadership.

Any class-based vision of social transformation in relation to black women's poverty must centralize gender and sexuality. The PPC had the potential to be more effective had it included gender in its analytic frameworks and practical strategies to address poverty in America, particularly within black communities. My turn to the class-based politics of the PPC is not only about recovering the muted voices of women in the PPC but also about understanding the significance and value of a liberative gender and sexual politics within class-based approaches related to black women's poverty. Simply put, the PPC tried to combat poverty but didn't consider the ways in which black women's poverty intersects with gender and sexuality. A progressive class-based politics for poor black women will challenge the prevailing black gender and sexual relations, which can lead to a revival of the PPC's norms of inclusion and participation with and for poor persons in America across racial groups.

THE BLACK CHURCH AND THE
SOUTHERN CHRISTIAN LEADERSHIP CONFERENCE

Class does intersect with gender and sexuality. Because of the increased feminization of black poverty, failing to address questions of gender and sexuality will compromise even anti-racist, class-based black politics. When one takes seriously the class, gender, and sexual dimensions of poor black women's continual economic oppression, one is able to reenvision effective strategies to ameliorate and eradicate their impoverished status.

When I speak of gender and sexuality, I am not narrowly referring to women, sexism, or the act of sex. I am more broadly referring to the social and cultural engendered experiences of women and men, cultural definitions of womanhood and manhood, and the interconnections among race, gender, sexuality, age, class, and other forms of oppression. We must critically examine the gender and sexual politics of the PPC, which naturally leads to an examination of the gender politics of the SCLC and the black churches that initiated and led the movement.

My turn to the black churches and the SCLC is a critical turn to both the possibilities and limitations of the organization that spurred the PPC. The SCLC was born in the wake of the Civil Rights movement. In 1957 King invited approximately sixty male clergy to a meeting at Ebenezer Baptist Church in Atlanta. The initial goal of the SCLC was to privilege and employ nonviolent direct action as a primary method of desegregating bus systems across the South.

During its formative years, the SCLC struggled to collaborate with black churches and communities across the South. Only a few black churches possessed the moral courage to defy the South's white racist structures of power by affiliating themselves with the SCLC. Those few black churches that did were most vulnerable to retaliations such as bombings. Social activism for racial justice met fierce opposition from sociopolitical institutions such as law enforcement and organizations such as the Ku Klux Klan. Moreover, these few black churches also received extreme disapproval from their fellow black pastors, who worried that such radical activism would make all black churches future targets for retaliatory violence.

The SCLC's social advocacy of nonviolent protest and its direct methods (boycotts, sit-ins, and so on) proved to be controversial in both black and white communities. Many black community leaders maintained that "segregation should be challenged in the courts and that direct action excited white resistance, hostility, and violence."[1] Traditionally, black leadership emerged from the educated elite (such as ministers, professionals, teachers) who "spoke for and on behalf of the laborers, maids, 'farm-hands,' and working-poor."[2] Many of these black traditional leaders were uncertain and uneasy with including ordinary blacks, and even black youth, in protests such as boycotts and marches.

Moreover, the SCLC's belief that churches should be involved in political activism against social ills was deeply controversial. Many black and white ministerial leaders thought the responsibility of the church primarily entailed focusing on the spiritual and personal needs of the congregation. To some, the social-political activity of King and the SCLC was dangerous radicalism, a radicalism that compromised the safety and well-being of black communities in the South. As noted earlier, black churches were deeply torn over how social justice could be achieved for the black community. Unlike progressive voices such as King, conservative black leaders argued that "social transformation is progressive and piecemeal, achieved through the courts and reasoned legal argumentation."[3] The SCLC did not resonate with this conservative view of social transformation. Its leaders maintained that black communities must "forcefully demand that their human rights be honored by law" and that this would require "diverse methods, including direct action protests, boycotts, sit-ins, and legal recourse."[4]

Black Women Activists and the SCLC

While some black women civil rights activists, such as Septima Clark, aligned themselves with the SCLC, the SCLC was charged with gender and sexual oppression due to its sexist and heterosexist norms and practices. These oppressive norms affected the SCLC's ability to strategize about the "next steps" within the Civil Rights movement. In particular, the repression and absence of major black female activists hurt the organizational activities of the SCLC, which would inevitably affect the movement to organize the Poor People's Campaign. For instance, Clark realized that "the SCLC and King deployed a modified hierarchal approach where local people were involved upon the request of King or other Civil Rights forerunners." For Clark, this top-down approach discounted the need to cultivate the "agential capacities of the masses and also contributed to the increased violence that could erupt at some marches and protests." Clark's approach to successful movements for equality was grounded in a "democratic bottom-up understanding of how social change occurs." For Clark, a model of participatory activism was needed to enable and empower oppressed persons to exercise their political and educational power. She believed the traditional hierarchal approach of the SCLC "failed to honor and maximize the real power that the masses actually possessed when treated as co-partners" in the vision of the Civil Rights movement.[5]

Black female activists such as Clark contributed greatly to the nascent stages of the Civil Rights movement. While the SCLC focused on nonviolent demonstrations and direct-action methods, Rosetta Ross points out that Clark believed that an education component would empower blacks to exercise their political and educational power at the grassroots level.[6] She wanted blacks not only to participate in demonstrations but also to have the educational, political, and economic knowledge to manage the many obstacles associated with mass protest movements. For example, once blacks were given the right to vote, many of them were still dissuaded by legally implemented "literacy tests."[7] Blacks' ability to read had direct political consequences for the success of the direct protests and demonstrations associated with the Civil Rights movement. If blacks could not demonstrate literacy, their voting privileges were often rescinded when they went to the ballot box. When blacks could read, they were rarely disempowered or dissuaded when going to vote.[8] Clark, according to Ross, believed that "citizenship education was an equally important strategy to secure the success of the Civil Rights Movement."[9] This program could create socially conscious individuals who knew how to confront the unpredictable impediments that ensued after civil rights legislative gains.

While Clark certainly contributed to the strategic goals and successes of the SCLC, gender inequality hindered women activists—such as Clark—from making their full strategic contribution to the SCLC and the larger civil rights struggle. She complained that women's opinions about the strategies and tactics to be used in achieving civil rights aims were not valued as the opinions of male leaders within the group. Clark observed that the men of the SCLC did not respect women activists as equal partners alongside male leaders within the movement.[10] The inequitable treatment of women definitely was a key weakness of the Civil Rights movement.

Ella Baker was another black female civil rights activist who bemoaned the gender bias within the SCLC and the Civil Rights movement. Hired as the first staff person of the SCLC, Baker was at the forefront of the voter registration activities of the SCLC as well as the formation of the Student Non-Violent Coordinating Committee (SNCC), which galvanized and mobilized youth participation in the direct-action strategies and mass protests of the Civil Rights movement.

Baker resigned from the SCLC in 1960, criticizing its male-led methods. She believed that charismatic leadership was neither the answer to the Civil Rights movement nor effective.[11] The social movement did not need a spokesperson to speak on behalf of black people. Rather, she argued, protests against civil rights restrictions must employ "a model of participatory democracy in order to locate the success of the movement in the individuals that make up the movement" rather than in a few handpicked leaders.[12] Her idea of participatory democracy was grounded in three major tenets: (1) the centrality of the social movement as a grassroots movement that empowers local people to exercise their educational abilities and social decision-making powers; (2) the minimization of hierarchy and its associated prerequisite that expertise and professionalism is the basis for leadership; and (3) a call for direct action in response to fear and intellectual detachment.[13] Most important, Baker refused to let sexism determine who was qualified to lead within black communities.

With such strong female voices overtly challenging sexism, an inevitable collision of race and gender issues ensued in the SCLC. Black women leaders such as Clark and Baker not only waged a valiant battle against sexism within their communities, but were also openly critical of black male leadership, speaking with "remarkable candor about intra-racial gender tensions."[14] Gender dynamics would intensify and become more palpable during the Civil Rights movement, especially after 1965 with the emergence of black nationalism and the fledgling black feminist liberation movement. In fact, this collision of gender and race would eventually give rise to radical black feminist discourse and practice within the Civil Rights movement.

Paula Giddings accurately described the 1960s as a "masculine decade" within black communities, a masculine focus that black women activists would resist and challenge.[15] Black nationalist discourse included an explicit message about the destructive aspects of feminism and black women's quest for liberation. For many male black nationalists, "feminism was a white female middle-class movement that retarded racial unity and drew black women away from their more urgent work, which included eradicating racial oppression."[16] This black nationalist sentiment shows up in the ideologies and practices of the largely male-led Civil Rights movement. An unfortunate illustration of the overall marginalization of black women in the black liberation struggle (despite their dedicated and persistent involvement in it) is disclosed in the decision on the part of civil rights leaders not to allow a black woman to speak at the March on Washington in 1963.

Women Marginalized at the March on Washington

Anna Arnold Hedgeman describes her feelings about the male-dominated civil rights leadership and her experiences as the only woman on the planning committee for the March on Washington. The planning committee for the march included the "Big Six": A. Phillip Randolph and Martin Luther King (SCLC), Roy Wilkins (NAACP), James Farmer (CORE), and Whitney Young (National Urban League).[17] While Dorothy Height, president of the National Council of Negro Women (NCNW) was the sixth leader of the Big Six, she often lamented how the other five leaders devalued and discounted her insights and contributions concerning decisions.[18]

The architects (the Big Six) of the march on Washington planned to allow the wives of the civil rights leaders and a few other black women freedom fighters to sit on the dais. An arbitrary "Tribute to Women" was added to the program to give the appearance that women's contributions were recognized. It included Rosa Parks, Daisy Bates, Diane Nash, and Gloria Richardson, who were introduced but were not allowed to speak or even march in the vanguard with the male leaders.[19] Not one of the women directly involved in the movement (such as Baker, Clark, or even Height), who had literally risked their bodies and lives, was invited to the White House to meet with President Kennedy following the march. Women within the March on Washington pleaded for inclusion.

Photographs of the March show Dr. Height, the head of a major organization for black women, sitting off to the side and invisible to the public. Some of the women such as Hedgeman were so offended and insulted by these overt actions of gender injustice that they refused to attend the March. After the March, under the auspices of the NCNW, many women met as a group in an "After the March, What?" session at a local hotel, which was denounced by many male civil rights leaders. In fact, a few black female leaders remarked that male civil rights leaders told the women that they couldn't hold the rally.[20]

Although Marian Wright Edelman initially provided the idea of the PPC to Dr. King, the actual advice of women was sought only after the PPC's vision of Resurrection City started to fail miserably. In fact, many scholars attribute the SCLC's small turn-around to Edelman. In early planning for the PPC, the SCLC's leaders created a set of anti-poverty demands that were too broad and unrealistic. At the end of June they had narrowed their priority list, identifying four items as central: food, jobs, housing, and welfare. This revised priority list was, in large part, due to Edelman, who was no newcomer to Civil Right activism in relation to poverty.[21] Edelman had worked for the NAACP Legal Defense Fund and was part of a 1967 team of investigators that had studied poverty in twelve counties in Mississippi.[22] That survey disclosed evidence of abject poverty among rural blacks in Mississippi (hunger, malnutrition, and even starvation), which reflected the broader impoverished condition of more than one million poor blacks living in the rural backwaters of the American South in the 1960s.[23] In short, this twenty-nine-year-old African American female lawyer was one of few leaders who brought clarity and coherence to a campaign that was failing and demoralized. Edelman can be partially credited with restoring the campaign's credibility as the SCLC leaders strategized on how to end the PPC.

Concerns of Gender and Sexual Equality

The persistence of gender inequality within black communities under-mined the fact that improving the status of black communities required improving the status of black women, which meant paying attention to matters of gender. In fact, Height comments that her concern about civil rights leaders was that "there was not equal concern about women and gender as there was about race."[24] She reminded black communities that while leadership was male, the backbone of the Civil Rights movement was most certainly women and youth.

Women and girls were present in large numbers throughout some of the most dramatic moments of the Civil Rights movement. Many images of the Civil Rights movement disclose the record number of women who endured police brutality for the sake of black equality. For example, one can turn to a "1964 image of Mississippi beautician Vera Piggy styling hair while educating her customers about voter registration."[25] There is also a 1963 photo of students at Florida A&M University, a historically black college, depicting hundreds of people, mostly women, "who are answering court charges for protesting against segregated movie theaters."[26]

Six of the so-called Little Rock Nine, black teenagers whose lives were threatened when they integrated the Arkansas city's high schools in 1957, were young women. Furthermore, a host of women challenged bus segre-gation before Rosa Parks. In order to support the bus boycotts, four black Montgomery women arranged car pools and even sold pies to raise money for alternate transportation.[27] These "women chose to boycott the Mont-gomery bus systems for more than a year until the Supreme Court upheld a lower court's ruling in favor of these four black Montgomery women who had refused to comply with bus segregation—and this was months before Rosa Parks made her famous ride."[28]

Homophobia in the Movements

The SCLC's gender and sexual politics had sexist overtones and also possessed heterosexist proclivities. Civil rights master strategist Bayard Rustin, a gay black man, organized for King one of the largest nonviolent protests ever held in the United States: the 1963 March on Washington. In 1956, Rustin arrived at Montgomery to assist with the nascent bus boycott movement. When Rustin arrived, King was still deeply ambivalent about nonviolent resistance as the method of the Civil Rights movement. In fact, King possessed guns in his home and kept guards posted at his door. How-ever, Rustin "persuaded King and other boycott leaders to fully embrace nonviolence, even teaching them Gandhian nonviolent direct protest."[29] It seems clear that Rustin deeply influenced King at a critical point in the

Civil Rights movement. One could even argue that Rustin helped mold King into the international symbol of peace and nonviolence he would become.

However, Rustin was silenced, beaten, and ostracized despite his achievements for the movement. He was fired from important positions within the movement because he was openly gay in a severely homophobic era. Within the leadership of the SCLC, there was often vehement resistance because of Rustin's sexual identity.[30] Nonetheless, Rustin was a central figure in ending legal segregation in America.

The sexist and heterosexist inclinations of the SCLC were part of a broader construction and articulation of black masculinity that tended to be hyper-heterosexual and often expressed itself as anti woman and anti gay. The black nationalist movement of the 1960s refused to acknowledge sexual variety in black communities because such variety was thought to undermine, in part, the "essence" of the black man. Black masculinity communicated for many black men their sense of "headship" in family, community, and church. Black cultural acceptance of homophobia is linked to an acceptance of traditional notions of womanhood-manhood and an embrace of Western, especially Christian, anti-homosexual prejudices.[31] Black women were interpreted as betraying black men by speaking publicly about the pervasive sexism they endured in the 1960s. Similarly, black homosexuals and lesbians were seen as an affront to the quest for healthy black families and for a regulated and normalized black heterosexuality.

From the 1960s to contemporary times, black masculinity is constructed in a particular way. Black manhood is constructed as hyper-masculine, and black homosexuality, lesbianism, or bisexuality are the antitheses of authentic black masculinity. Johnnetta Cole and Beverly Guy-Sheftall write:

> It's a black machismo that is very much related to images of athletes, entertainment, and rap artists. It's supposed to represent what it is to be a man in the black community, and that is to be anti-gay, physically very strong, and to demonstrate male sexual prowess. It's a cluster of myths regarding the black male, and embedded in the heart of it is a hatred of people who are specifically gay and lesbian. That was the model that was held up and that many people bought into.[32]

Such sexual politics characterized the black cultural politics of the 1960s. James Baldwin, for example, endured vicious attacks in relation to his sexuality as a gay man. There was also a Back to Africa movement that entailed various myths about the origins of black sexuality. One of the myths Black America perpetuated about itself is that same-sex desires and relationships are alien to African cultures and that such practices within black communities are a manifestation of white pathological behaviors.

There has been a voluminous amount of literature challenging this view, arguing that there has been a diverse range of sexual behaviors and practices in Africa.[33] For instance, social and cultural anthropologist Gloria Wekker does not use homosexual, lesbian, heterosexual, or bisexual categories in her analysis when discussing the complex issue of African sexualities. As an Afro-Surinamese anthropologist, Wekker suggests that scholars can best analyze same-sex behavior cross-culturally by foregoing Western categories such as heterosexual, homosexual, lesbian, and bisexual, which have particular meanings in the United States context. She describes the institution of *matiism* among the African Diaspora in Paramaribo, Suriname. *Mati* is the Sranan Tongo word used to describe "women who have sexual relations with other women but who typically also will have had or still have relationships with men, simultaneously."[34] In discussing this institution among Creole working-class women in Suriname, Wekker avoids using homosexual or lesbian vocabulary because it does not adequately describe the complexity of these women's sexual practices. These women consider their sexual relations with other women as pleasurable but would not identify with any of the traditional categories of sexuality in the West. Rather, Wekker honors the diverse sexual universe these working-class women inhabit. One can infer from Wekker's study that sexual behaviors and practices have various meanings in different cultures.

Wekker's analysis of gender and sexuality stands in stark contrast to the black sexual politics of the SCLC, which was undergirded by a hegemonic black masculinity. Such hegemonic black masculinity is fundamentally a relational construct. It expresses "hierarchal power relations of a racialized system of sexism that frames the multiple expressions of masculinity and femininity available to black men and women."[35] It is defined through its difference from such persons as women and gay men.

The Nature of Black Masculinity

There are also several well-known cultural standards of black masculinity. First, "real" black men are primarily defined as not being like women. Real black men are expected to be forceful, rational, responsible, and willing to exert authority, qualities that women presumably lack. Second, real black men have control over women. Within this logic, men who are seen as befriending women of their racial or ethnic group without any real authority over them suffer a loss of manhood. Third, real men exercise complete control over their emotions with women. Hence, real men must be seen as non-emotive, aggressive, and physically strong. Fourth, real men are initiated into manhood through sexual intercourse with women. These men embody the benefits of adult masculinity: the ability to control women's bodies.[36]

Such understandings of black masculinity deeply affect poor black women. Historically, black women have needed protection against the sexual advances of white men. However, such hyper-masculinity makes black women even more vulnerable, particularly poor black women within segregated inner cities. Within the urban context of violence and poverty, many black women choose to support black men at all costs. Whether ignoring abuse or caring for their children with little help from the fathers, poor black women are often forced to struggle to care for themselves and their offspring. Poor black women continue to endure the problem of black male sexual dominance due to ideas of black masculinity, which often force poor black women to become mythical superwomen.

However, there is a contradiction related to the problem of hegemonic black masculinity. Black men who embody such masculinity simultaneously depend on women for their physical survival. They often depend on their girlfriends and mothers of their children for financial support.[37] This establishes a potentially dangerous situation for poor black women if their black male partners are abusive and controlling toward them, which compromises poor black women and their children socially and economically.

In part, this form of hegemonic black masculinity hampered the gender and sexual politics within the civil rights struggle, which influenced the class-based efforts of the SCLC (and eventually the PPC). As we will see when turning to the Poor People's Campaign, the failure to attend to issues of gender and sexuality diminishes and vitiates the success of any anti-racist, class-based movement for economic justice.

THE LAST CRUSADE:
THE EMERGENCE OF THE POOR PEOPLE'S CAMPAIGN
MOVEMENT

The PPC wasn't attentive to how the inclusion of gender and sexuality could have strengthened its class-based efforts to address the growing economic inequities and inequalities that deeply affected black women and their children. By 1967, Martin Luther King, Jr., was viewed as the most dangerous radical in America, a threat to America's way of life. That same year King underwent a painful reassessment of his long-held beliefs and principles in relation to overcoming white supremacy.[38] His earlier convictions were that white racism could be overcome by appealing to the practical force of Christian love and nonviolence that people saw as ultimately guiding America. However, with the emergence and contradictions of the Vietnam war, King concluded that "our only hope today lies in our ability to recapture the revolutionary spirit and go out into a sometimes hostile world declaring eternal hostility to poverty, racism, and militarism."[39] King's reassessment of American racism came out of his realization that the Civil

Rights movement was at an impasse. Although equal opportunity and equal constitutional rights for black communities were irrefutably essential to the black freedom movement, black persons also "needed the economic and cultural resources to take advantage of the recently won political freedoms. King quickly realized that the economic fate of American blacks was intricately tied to other poor persons across racial categories in this country and abroad."[40] While King had always been sensitive to poverty as a race leader, he developed a broader vision of the nature of poverty in America and the strategies needed to address such impoverishment.

The Changing Economy

As discussed earlier, millions of unskilled workers lost their jobs as the American economy shifted from an industrial economy to a post-industrial economy. King understood the implications of this economic reality for unskilled workers during the 1960s and 1970s. Historian Gerald McKnight writes about King's realization:

In the steel, auto, meat-packing, and tobacco industries, electrical and paper manufacturing, and mining, new technologies wiped out millions of jobs. And blacks were often severely affected. Technology was color-blind but blacks had been restricted to the dangerous and dirty unskilled and semi-skilled jobs that were now most at risk.[41]

Without attention to economy, racial justice would become more elusive and unattainable. In addition, the urban riots of the 1960s reflected the chronic conditions of a black underclass whose poverty was often more severe because it intersected with racial and gender oppression. King knew that the racial freedom movement had to address strategically the economic duress of an American underclass in order for black equality and freedom to truly be possibilities. King had discovered "the missing piece in the black freedom struggle."[42]

Under King's leadership, the SCLC decided to take up issues of economy as central to the agenda of the Civil Rights movement. In 1963, King held a meeting with his staff to brainstorm on how to dramatize poverty and its social costs in America. Marian Wright Edelman put forth an idea to stage sit-ins in Washington at key government offices.[43] She advocated that the "nation's invisible poor needed to camp out on the officials' doorstep until federal power promised to take action to eradicate these deplorable conditions."[44] This sit-in would be a massive civil disobedience campaign called the Poor People's Campaign, scheduled for spring 1968. It would comprise poor persons across racial lines to demand an Economic Justice Bill of Rights to improve their economic opportunities.

The protestors planned to demand that President Lyndon Johnson and Congress give the poor better access to jobs, healthcare, and decent housing. The campaign was intended to be a peaceful gathering of poor people from all racial communities across the nation. The plan was for protestors to march through the capital and visit various federal agencies in hopes of getting Congress to pass substantial anti-poverty legislation.[45] They would not leave until Congress fulfilled their demands. They wanted nothing less than economic justice.

Organization of the Campaign

The PPC was a radical departure from previous SCLC projects. First, this movement was not advocating solely for black equality. The leaders of the PPC envisioned "bringing to Washington thousands of the nation's disadvantaged in an interracial alliance that embraced rural and ghetto blacks, Appalachian whites, Mexican Americans, Puerto Ricans, and Native Americans."[46] In launching the "poor people's army," King was proposing nothing less than a radical transformation of the Civil Rights movement into a populist crusade, demanding the redistribution of economic and political power. America's most celebrated civil rights leader was now focusing on class issues in order to force national leaders to respond to the needs of an ignored underclass population.[47]

The campaign broadened its social and racial base and foregrounded the ongoing struggles for jobs and justice in the North. It transformed the Civil Rights movement into a radical crusade for economic redistribution, which was and remains a radical threat to America's class system and dominant institutions. By 1966, King concluded that the Civil Rights movement's most stubborn impediments "were economic rather than legal, and tied much more closely to questions of class than issues of race."[48] Race and class are intertwined and reinforce structures of unequal power. The leadership of the PPC recognized racism's malignant kinship with the nation's class-based power structures. The aim of the PPC's massive protest was to "move the federal government from guaranteeing legal protections for civil and voting rights to spending billions of dollars for full employment, income guarantees, and a massive reconstruction of urban communities."[49]

The PPC sought to forge coalitions across lines of race and class. The dreams and hopes of the PPC were to unite and mobilize organized and unorganized workers, the unemployed, welfare-reliant mothers, and the poor of all racial and ethnic groups. The PPC demanded adequate incomes for women whose primary labor remained childrearing, as well as guaranteed jobs and decent wages for both men and women. In seeking to forge these progressive coalitions, the PPC confronted complex dilemmas of race and class. Widening class stratification increasingly complicated the notion of a black "community," which had ramifications when turning to a black middle class to supply leadership (and even resources) for the race struggle. Moreover, despite similarly limited economic opportunities for poor persons across racial lines, racial tensions and strife continued to be present among the diverse poor of different ethnic groups and communities within the American underclass. Could this movement foster solidarity among people across lines of class and forge sustainable alliances with members of all races affected by economic inequalities?

The PPC sought the inclusion of blacks within the American political economy in alliance with poor whites, recognizing that this strategy would redefine the poverty question, American power, and basic opportunity in fundamental ways. The PPC's central insight was that poverty is caused by a lack of economic power and that poor people (across all socioeconomic and cultural backgrounds) need to be mobilized politically to realize the nation's promises of economic opportunity. The PPC also attempted to reconcile necessary race-specific programs with full employment and income-support policies that would benefit all Americans. For example, King did not want blacks to be perceived as receiving preferential treatment in public programs; he realized that "such a perception would be detrimental to economic gains for blacks."[50] Therefore, the PPC sought to expand the Civil Rights movement from a black freedom struggle to a human rights struggle. It sought sweeping reforms in employment, education, welfare, housing, and wages for poor persons of all cultural backgrounds.

The Leadership of Ralph Abernathy and Jesse Jackson

Weeks before the march was to take place, King was assassinated. A cadre of black ministers, including Ralph Abernathy and Jesse Jackson, decided they would pick up where King had left off, announcing that the Poor People's March on Washington would be held. Thousands of people participated in the march on May 12, 1968. As he led the demonstrators, Abernathy stated, "We come with an appeal to open the doors of America to the almost 50 million Americans who have not been given a fair share of America's wealth and opportunity, and we will stay until we get it."[51] A week later, protestors erected a settlement of tents on the National Mall, where they camped for six weeks. Jackson became mayor of the encampment, which was called Resurrection City.

Resurrection City was to be a semi-permanent camp of the nation's poor that would serve as a reminder to the nation (and government officials) that the Great Society's war on poverty had not produced significant tangible results. Over a decade later, Abernathy would recall his vision for the city as the embodiment of hope, a model of a just society:

We would set up a model for the rest of the nation to emulate. Everyone would live together in peace and mutual respect. . . . We would have people of all races, ethnic backgrounds, and religious beliefs. Since everyone would be poor, there would be no greed or envy. . . . And our business would be to go from government agency to government agency, representing the poor, speaking out for their interests, asking for several concrete things from our government, the richest nation in the world.[52]

Abernathy's model for the PPC's city of hope was reminiscent of the early Puritan fathers, who left their English homeland to found a "city upon a hill" to serve as a moral example to the nation. He believed that Resurrection City would capture the conscience of the nation and galvanize support behind the campaign's goal to eradicate poverty and extend hope to the helpless and frustrated.[53]

Resurrection City was "a city of A-frame huts made of plywood and canvas that took shape between the white marbled formality of the Lincoln Memorial and the Washington Monument."[54] Almost all the building materials were donated. Volunteer labor from church and neighborhood groups added to this city of protest and hope. In addition to residential shelters, the city "possessed eating facilities, toilets, medical and child care centers, a meeting hall, and planned space for Freedom Schools."[55] This city even had its own zip code. The SCLC leaders and residents hoped this city would awaken the conscience of the nation to act in light of its poor neighbors. In fact, SCLC leaders hoped that this massive movement of civil disobedience would provide the type of shock value that occurred during protests over segregation; it would wake American citizens from their slumber of abundance.[56]

However, the PPC did not fare as well as anticipated. While it achieved some small victories, Resurrection City was overall a dismal failure for a number of reasons. Foremost, the SCLC was taking on the task of building a city from scratch and administering to the needs of approximately three thousand persons.[57] This undertaking was without precedence in the history of American protest movements. Resurrection City also "suffered from the cultural attitudes of many young blacks who saw the city as nothing more than a party. Thus, Resurrection City shifted in demographics over time."[58] It went from "a gathering of multicultural people who had been trained in nonviolent protest to a gathering of young blacks (many unemployed and many associated with gangs) under twenty-five who saw the city as a place to have fun."[59]

Another setback was the power struggle that persisted within the leadership ranks of the SCLC and the PPC. For example, Ralph Abernathy never received legitimation as the new civil rights leader of the SCLC in the wake of King's death. When Abernathy sought counsel from Bayard Rustin, other male SCLC leaders attacked Abernathy. Rustin was not liked by other male leaders within the organization for being vocal about his identity as a black gay man. Jesse Jackson also encountered resistance from many of the male leaders. Jackson was seen as courting media coverage in order to gain greater visibility. People thought that he was undermining and undercutting Abernathy's authority and that of other veteran leaders. These personal antagonisms were exacerbated by "the growing combination of torrential rains and chronic mismanagement within Resurrection City."[60] According to the FBI, Resurrection City had become an "unalloyed version of a modern day Sodom and Gomorrah," which could be characterized by "wholesale lawlessness, violence, rape, petty theft," and so on.[61] So, it seems that the PPC's biggest problems was not money; its big problem was leadership.

While the vision of the PPC sought to inaugurate an analysis of poverty in America that was based more on race and class, this movement, in part, also failed because it was not sensitive to how its gender and sexual politics undermined its effectiveness and success. I do not argue that such gender and sexual politics directly resulted in the PPC's failure; rather, they greatly contributed to its failure.

The PPC's continuing strategies disclosed an absence of consideration given to issues of gender and sexuality within its anti-poverty strategies. As noted earlier, Height's advice concerning black women's socioeconomic realities could have been instructive for PPC leadership of the type of strategies needed as PPC evolved. Black women (and women in general, for that matter) experience poverty in qualitatively different ways than black men do. Poor black women are the caretakers of America's poorest group: black children. They also experience wage inequality that is more chronic than white women and black men. Black women leaders such as Height, Baker, and Clark have always highlighted the troubling poverty statistic that women and children have been disproportionately represented as the "poorest of the poor." The continued repression and devaluation of black women's political leadership certainly contributed to the declining campaign against poverty, as these voices were unable to provide such perspectives in a way that shaped the movement from the ground up.

The PPC and Women's Concerns

It was noted earlier that one of the demands of the PPC was an adequate income for women whose primary labor was childrearing. The PPC also sought to address and strengthen welfare policies. However, as indicated in the previous chapter, arguing for the continued presence of welfare policies is insufficient unless it is accompanied by a deconstruction of how such policies perpetuate structural violence on poor black women. The sexual and gender politics within the PPC did not enable leaders to study how welfare regulates and controls the bodies and lives of women in America.

In addition, because welfare policy is deeply connected to domestic violence among women in general, the leadership of the PPC needed to address how hegemonic masculinities reinforce such violence toward women. Such issues for poor black women (and poor women in general) were left unaddressed, in large part due to the assumptions and values that undergirded the PPC's male leadership. A better grasp of the issues affecting poor women could have led to different strategies within the PPC, both in terms of leadership and policy recommendations.

The PPC could have experienced greater success had it critically reflected upon and modified its traditional understandings of gender and sexual politics. The presence of hegemonic black masculinity continues to undergird black communities and black church spaces today and hinders most black churches from constructing a more progressive outlook. For example, the controversial case of Eddie Long, accused in 2010 of sexual misconduct by four young men, discloses the unhealthy and destructive politics that continues to plague the Black Church. The media and other black clergy did not concentrate on clergy abuse but instead on the "pathological" nature of same-sex relations. It took a while for commentators, black scholars, and some members of the black clergy to decry how the media implicitly pathologizes same-sex relationships.

While I have no intention of proving or disproving Long's guilt or innocence, this example reveals the absence of a view of healthy sexuality within black communities, the Black Church, and our larger society. Moving forward, black churches and political organizations associated with them (such as SCLC-type organizations) must commit to deconstructing unhealthy masculinities in order to offer a more life-giving black sexual politics. Such a politics can aid black churches and reshape conversation surrounding black women's poverty. Womanist scholars such as Kelly Brown Douglas offer healthier perspectives of sexuality in relation to the Black Church. These voices deserve to be heard and engaged within black churches.[62]

These conversations are essential if a Black Church–led PPC is to be resuscitated, revived, and emboldened. If the Black Church is to be a community of transcendence for poor black women, it must honestly address oppressive black masculinities and their implications for poor black women. A new PPC movement must also restore the original norms of inclusion and participation with and for the poor in their own liberation from economic deprivation. The PPC movement is unfinished business; however, it can be revived with more effective leadership. The Black Church in America can contribute to an economy of hope for the poor.

6

A New Kind of Prosperity Gospel

A new Poor People's Campaign has the potential to introduce a class-based, multi-ethnic movement for economic justice. It could also examine the idea of prosperity as both personal and structural, involving both individual and communal flourishing. This vision of prosperity moves beyond the narrow, individualistic market understanding of prosperity: that one's faithfulness leads to wealth. Yet how can we talk about individual success if a person is not given the means and tools to succeed? The PPC's focus on how inequitable structures and unfair economic institutions impede the poor's progress has been sadly neglected in black churches' current responses to black women's poverty. Its norms of inclusion of and participation by the poor must be integrated into anti-poverty approaches.

As discussed earlier, faith-based initiatives rarely address or challenge how exploitative economic institutions perpetuate cycles of impoverishment for poor persons across racial categories. Inequities within the American political economy continue to frustrate poor people's actions toward flourishing and thriving. While I do not advocate a wholesale rejection of faith-based initiatives or even faith-based entrepreneurship, I do find most woefully lacking. They tend to dismiss or ignore the real inequalities associated with free-market systems and institutions that keep the poor disenfranchised and economically disempowered. The Black Church–led PPC took account of such systemic inequities. Moreover, this Black Church–led movement worked with a vision of prosperity rooted in *class-based* efforts to eradicate poverty.

Many contemporary black churches have lost this class-based vision of economic justice for the poor. Instead, they articulate and promote a prosperity gospel theology that reinforces neo-liberal free-market values. The current prosperity gospel thrust ignores the vast complexities and contradictions associated with wealth and prosperity in our market society and their negative effects on the poor.

The Black Church *can* fashion a more complete understanding of prosperity within the context of the market forces in America and around the globe. Many current understandings of prosperity within the Black Church are inadequate because they do not consider how individualistic notions of prosperity undermine communal well-being and flourishing. Yet, the Black Church *can* become a religious site that provides a "home" where poor black women can truly experience hope and flourishing. The Black Church *can* also resurrect a broad class-based vision of justice.

However, to do so these institutions must reevaluate their current religious ideologies, including prosperity gospel teaching, that support the interests of those in power or those who benefit from grossly unequal economic arrangements. Black churches need a more expanded, holistic concept of prosperity that includes an interplay between individual fulfillment and communal well-being and fosters social trust, compassion, inclusion, and participation among all poor persons. A more holistic understanding of prosperity can offer cultural and religious resources to address the amelioration of poverty, especially among black women.

THE POVERTY OF
PROSPERITY GOSPEL THEOLOGY

Like any other institution the Black Church evolves, grows, and changes over time. Much research indicates that it has developed into what I call a post–civil rights church. This does not refer to the end or culmination of the civil rights struggles for blacks, but rather to how black communities have evolved over the last four decades. They are now characterized by greater economic stratification and sociocultural differences; thus, bringing about change requires new methods. While earlier methods and strategies were expressed in racial terms, post–civil rights methods and strategies must be framed beyond purely racial terms (as did the PPC). Economic issues necessitate giving increasing importance to class, gender, and sexuality in order to address effectively the greater poverty of women. The Black Church of the twenty-first century must reexamine its language, its methods, and its strategies in relation to the *new ways* that race, class, gender, sexuality, and more converge to structure adversely the economic opportunities of poor black women.

Hope and black cultural renewal have always been important to the mission of the Black Church. This is an essential first step for blacks in order to empower them to transcend the racist logic and practices of white privilege. However, hope for "the least of these" within black communities (the black poor, especially black women) is often eclipsed by an insidious religious worldview that blames the poor for their own poverty. This religious worldview has gained ground over the last few decades, and this worldview is part of the prosperity gospel's theology.

Many black neo-Pentecostal and "word of faith" preachers teach their parishioners that wealth should be seen as part of their rightful inheritance as God's children. They encourage their congregants to "name and claim" God's promises of wealth and divine health for all Christians who have great faith. Such leaders correlate wealth with the quality of one's faith and obedience in God; wealth and health are the results of unwavering faith. Consequently, those who experience chronic illness or financial duress must lack faith in God's eternal promise of riches and abundance for God's children.

The Roots of the Prosperity Gospel

It is interesting to note that prosperity gospel theology is partly rooted in shifts within the American political economy and a growing American middle class. As indicated earlier, shifts in the American political economy (from an industrial to a post-industrial economy) created a growing American underclass. However, in the 1980s other economic shifts occurred that strengthened and expanded the middle and upper classes in this country. Many in the middle to upper class became beneficiaries of unprecedented financial prosperity that reached its economic zenith with the Clinton administration in the 1990s. As the black middle class grew, there was a need to affirm and reinforce its economic and social achievements, especially as a black underclass was also increasing in number. Prosperity gospel teachings were able to reinterpret the quest of the American dream as central to Christian experience. For a growing black middle class, this reinterpretation affirmed people's continual material pursuit of wealth without any attention to inequitable structures within their own communities.

The prosperity gospel movement introduced a new breed of leaders. During the Civil Rights movement, primarily Baptist and African Methodist Episcopal (AME) clergy were at the forefront. Many of the direct protests and campaigns of the Civil Rights movement were fashioned and led by these denominational leaders. While most black Pentecostal clergy placed more emphasis theologically on personal piety and the coming *eschaton*, Baptist and AME clergy had a more expansive concept of religion, which included how black persons could experience cultural and material flourishing and thriving within current social systems. However, beginning in the 1980s a shift occurred within the Black Church. With the influx of young, upwardly mobile middle-class people into Pentecostal and charismatic denominations, a brand of neo-Pentecostalism emerged. These neo-Pentecostals were not interested in waiting on the hereafter or focusing on the coming *eschaton*. Members of this new middle class were preoccupied with how to understand their faith in light of their quest for the individual success promised by the American dream. Prosperity gospel theology attempted not only to help members of this new group connect their faith with their increased wealth but also to explain why the poor continued to experience deprivation: lack of faith.

In addition, "word-of-faith" preachers also became more visible and audible in the 1980s. Black sociologist Shayne Lee explores the prosperity gospel teachings of word-of-faith preachers. Started by Kenneth Hagin, Sr., and a small group of white ministers in the 1970s, word-of-faith teachings assert that "Christians have the power to control their physical well-being and financial fortunes through their faith."[1] A primary assumption undergirding word-of-faith teachings is that the death and resurrection of Jesus Christ grants Christians total victory over their lives, which includes divine (perfect) health and financial prosperity. Poor health and financial duress, therefore, result from lack of faith or inappropriate biblical principles. Word-of-faith or "word" preachers contend that "once believers strengthen their faith by memorizing and confessing scriptures, they are able to live in total victory and control their physical and financial fate."[2] Simply put, word-of-faith teachings argue that God wants all Christians to experience financial prosperity. It is a "divine right."[3]

Instead of advocating for voting registration, direct protests, boycotts, and other forms of social action historically associated with black churches, "word" ministries teach members that "poverty is a curse from the devil and the power to transform one's oppressive realities resides in a person's measure of faith."[4] With great faith, a believer can be set free from impoverishment and able to take his or her "rightful place" in the kingdom of God.

Having grown up in a Pentecostal tradition (COGIC), I remember sitting in many churches that taught this central proposition. A prosperity gospel's answer to poverty is to strengthen one's faith and to believe those biblical promises that preachers interpret as pro wealth. Prosperity gospel's answer to poverty is for faithful Christians to give money to local churches so that God can "open the windows of heaven and pour out a blessing that a person doesn't even have room to receive," a saying often repeated within black churches. This theology has been attractive to members of the black middle and upper classes who need to affirm their financial prosperity as Christians, but it also provides a glimmer of hope to black working and poor communities who suffer from continual deprivation.

It would be difficult to find a black church that is not affected by prosperity gospel teachings, even though those teachings do a disservice to the poor by identifying their poverty as caused by their lack of faith. Economic facts belie these teachings. In the United States, poverty across racial groups has deep roots in systemic problems associated with shifts in the economy as well as the exploitative economic practices of market forces. Inequitable structural arrangements within the American political economy continue to exacerbate impoverishment.

Shortcomings of the Prosperity Gospel

Prosperity gospel teachings enable affluent persons, including multinational corporations and their CEOs, to justify their extreme wealth in religious terms, linking God's favor to their prosperity. Consequently, such corporations and CEOs are never held accountable for any exploitative policies that enable them to acquire wealth. For instance, the absence of a living wage grows the pocketbooks of the rich at the expense of working-class and underclass populations around the world. Grossly underpaid laborers around the world are often exploited for the company's "bottom line." Prosperity gospel teachings basically ignore the source and means of such profit. Unfair labor practices and wages are never considered. This understanding of how advanced capitalist societies function hides any possibilities to contest such economic oppression.

A theology that celebrates wealth based on faith alone cannot effectively challenge the ways in which economic arrangements are built on the backs of the poor, reinforcing and intensifying their impoverishment. Great faith simply does not improve the economic fortunes of those deprived of opportunity. Great faith does not challenge and alter the structures that keep masses of people in chronic poverty. Great faith doesn't answer the problems of poverty faced by black women. The prosperity gospel represents a very unsophisticated understanding of world markets and the exploitation of the labor and energies of the poor of the world.

Focusing on individual agency also does not consider how Western imperialism and capitalism perpetuate global poverty. For example, black prosperity gospel preacher Creflo Dollar's focus on individual agency does not consider how Western prosperity may derive from the equivalent of slave labor in sweatshops in South Asia.[5] His teaching on faith and financial success does not identify how the exploitative practices of multinational corporations reinforce cycles of poverty that entrap and exacerbate the deprivation of the poor. Instead, his teachings view poverty as the product of demonic oppression, a spiritual dis-ease to be conquered through prayer and tithing.[6]

Moreover, prosperity gospel preachers in the United States ignore or are "completely unaware of how their teachings are inapplicable to Christians in poverty-stricken nations such as Tanzania, Guatemala, Kenya, or Afghanistan who have few opportunities for social mobility."[7] There must be a profound restructuring of these societies to make individual agency possible.[8] For those who are wretchedly poor and uneducated in poor parts of Africa or Asia, opportunities to self-actualize and attain financial greatness are limited or nonexistent, no matter how much faith they have.[9] In other words, if the prosperity gospel's teachings were universally true, these assumptions would apply to all Christians in all cultural spaces. However, such teachings work well primarily in countries like the United States, where people have the ability to amass astronomical amounts of material wealth. Nonetheless, even in free-market societies, not everyone has the same level of opportunity: economic stratification hinders masses of people, including poor black women, from moving out of poverty.

TENSION BETWEEN HOPE AND BLAME

While I find the prosperity gospel theology's blaming of the poor deeply troubling, I do acknowledge the two-sided nature of this theology; although it is oppressive, it does provide contexts that motivate the poor. It often provides creative ways for black congregants to hope despite their experiences of devaluation and deprivation within this country. T. D. Jakes's emphasis on personal agency resonates with millions of Americans born and raised in the midst of free-market economics. For instance, Jakes's Woman Thou Art Loosed conference tries to persuade women, particularly the black women who make up the majority of his following, to be victorious within a system that attempts to subjugate them. He also encourages them to cultivate their own futures and to trust God and themselves to overcome any setbacks in their lives. This is a refreshing and empowering message for black women in an American culture that denigrates and devalues them and vilifies them based on their economic and cultural position. Many women attend Jakes's conferences and become resolute in their belief in themselves as subjects and moral actors with agency within their lives. Consequently, a certain complexity also characterizes the prosperity gospel. Unfortunately, while it attempts to aid persons to self-actualize, it simultaneously ignores those structural inequalities that undermine any attempt at self-actualization.

It is helpful to hold this potentially productive aspect of current prosperity gospel teachings in tension with its more destructive tendencies. While some prosperity gospel preachers do possess insincere, exploitative motives, other prosperity gospel teachers genuinely believe and embrace this interpretation of scripture. While Christian circles should encourage self-actualization and individual fulfillment, they should also denounce and resist inequitable arrangements that prevent such actualization. Unfortunately, the prosperity gospel message often fails to acknowledge that socioeconomic status is less an issue of faith and more an indication of structures that reproduce the unequal distributions of income, resources, and wealth. Jakes's conferences would profit from deeper insight into how economic structures affect black women's economic opportunities and how they can counter such structural arrangements as they exercise greater personal agency.

Simply put, Jakes's message does not acknowledge that working-class and poor women are often unable to make their efforts to flourish count within the larger market forces at work in their communities and the world. When I attended some of Jakes's meetings, I would often overhear black women (who attend this conference yearly) speak of their ongoing poverty with shame because they felt personally responsible. They believed it was a sign of their lack of faith, which is simply not true. Rather, they are entrapped by market forces that continually frustrate their attempts to thrive and flourish.

QUESTIONING THE CAPITALIST MOMENT

The religious worldview of the prosperity gospel movement does not question the "capitalist moment" in which we live. This moment, characterized by the commodification, exploitation, and maldistribution of resources, contributes to increasing poverty in America and abroad. It treats the human subject as a commodity. Labor, for example, is no longer seen as a human possession worthy of respect but rather as a commodity to be exchanged to maximize profit. Labor thus loses its humanizing element and is depersonalized—just one more commodity.

As noted earlier, advanced capitalism generally sponsors a morality that dehumanizes social relations, using them as a means to reach certain market goals. This "commodity fetishism" displaces social relationships by objectifying them as relationships among things (in this case, commodities and profit).

Such commodification of the human subject fosters economic exploitation and subjugation, particularly among those who are most vulnerable. As it dehumanizes social bonds, it privileges economic profit maximization as a primary social value. In fact, such capitalist values are even reified by disadvantaged, poor communities as values to be pursued and achieved. Within our nation and around the world, poor communities of color continue to experience chronic poverty due to these practices of commodification that fuel and sustain advanced capitalist economies.

The Capitalist Myth of Progress

Capitalist processes employ certain values in order to determine and shape economic outcomes. As indicated in the Introduction to this book, these "neo-liberal" attitudes can be seen in the myth of meritocracy, which maintains that an individual's success or failure is determined by that person's approach to work, savings, investment, and risk. However, this myth does not uncover the institutional and structural constraints that impede individual flourishing. Belief that an "invisible hand" regulates market transactions between individuals deems that state regulation (or government intervention) of the economy is both unnatural and harmful.

Neo-liberalism does not merely privilege an economic structure that resists government oversight and intervention; it is also a philosophy of success by means of individual action and merit. Individuals are responsible for their economic success or failure, not the markets or social, economic, or political structures. Individual merit and ambition are the hallmarks of responsible and deserving citizens; poor persons thus are irresponsible and undeserving, lacking in ambition and merit. Elite communities benefit while structural constraints perpetuate poverty among disadvantaged communities.

Described in this manner, it is difficult to see how our capitalist economy can be "progressive" or "democratizing" for the world's communities. Free-market advocates such as Milton Friedman and Dinesh D'Souza continue to tout our capitalist economy as securing greater wealth for nations around the world. For certain, capitalistic economies have contributed in some ways to world progress through travel, trade, migration, the sharing of cultural influences, and the dissemination of knowledge and understanding (including science and technology). However, globally poorer communities have *not been able to benefit from such gains* due to their lack of access to education, adequate housing, transportation, healthcare, and so on.

The Critique of Walter Benjamin

In large part the logic of capitalism is unquestioned; it is viewed as natural to American "progress" and is also seen as part of the civilizing process of underdeveloped nations around the world. Critical social theorist Walter Benjamin delineates exactly how deep inequities and inequalities are produced when the logic and practices of advanced capitalism are left unquestioned. In particular, Benjamin challenges the understanding of capitalism as progress, as a movement toward liberation and opportunity and away from barbarism and inequality. As a Jew under the Third Reich, Benjamin "confronted naked class struggle, rising fascism, and approaching war." The Third Reich was "rationalized by such state-sponsored violence with the logic of capitalist progress and modernity, an effective tool used to dominate."[10] For Benjamin, this logic of exploitation led to social and existential nightmares within Germany in which human beings (Jewish people and others) were conceptualized as chattel and commodities, dispensable elements of society.

Benjamin used an image in a painting to describe the dilemma associated with the modern reading of capitalism as progress. In 1921, he purchased a painting by Paul Klee entitled *Angelus Novus*, which metaphorically depicts the catastrophic and enigmatic character of capitalist history and its claim of progress. Benjamin describes the painting as follows:

> A Klee painting named "Angelus Novus" shows an angel looking as though he is about to move away from something he is fixedly contemplating. His eyes are staring, his mouth is open, his wings are spread. This is how one pictures the angel of history. His face is turned toward the past. Where we perceive a chain of events, he sees one single catastrophe which keeps piling wreckage upon wreckage and hurls it in front of his feet. The angel would like to stay, awaken the dead, and make whole what has been smashed. But a storm is blowing from Paradise; it has got caught in his wings with such violence that the angel can no longer close them. This storm irresistibly propels him into the future to which his back is turned, while the pile of debris before him grows skyward. This storm is what we call progress.[11]

In Klee's painting, the angel is presented with "eyes wide open." According to Benjamin, it is "scared of what it sees in its inverted view." The back of the angel "faces toward the future, although it is powerless against the storm of progress." Benjamin describes the angel as if "it longs to remain in the present for a while, actualizing historical redemption by awakening death and reconstructing the destroyed past."[12]

Benjamin's angel does not perceive capitalist history as following any course. Nor does it recognize capitalist history as progress. Instead, capitalist history is "frozen for an instant by the Angel's petrified look of horror."[13] Capitalist history is not a chain of progressive events, but a single catastrophe. The *Angelus Novus* radically questions the idea of capitalist progress and its technocratic ideologies and practices. For Benjamin, the angel discloses one enduring truth: *catastrophe is inevitable in every capitalist situation that does not question itself.*

Benjamin's reading of capitalism sheds important light on the effects of market forces on poor black women. It challenges both the systems of advanced capitalism and its linear movement of time, which always positions the present as progress. If capitalism is to be singularly interpreted as progress, then it cannot be understood in terms of inequalities or inequities. Considering capitalism as potentially catastrophic can, in part, uproot and shock understandings of the progressive present. It can awaken us to the "hell" of capitalist exploitation as failure instead of progress. It fuels alienation, marginalization, and repression for marginalized persons and especially for vulnerable communities, such as those of poor black women.

This disruption of capitalism's internal logic of progress is profoundly important. For example, free-market advocates in America see capitalism as an economic model that largely improves the material lives of persons around the world. According to that logic, market exchanges provide *all* persons with the opportunity to maximize their economic interests. This misguided conclusion is grounded in the assumption that capitalist history has been and is a linear movement of progress, which blinds one to capitalism's dark side, to the ways in which it fosters and exacerbates the gross inequities and inequalities of vulnerable populations. In fact, capitalism engenders the commodification and exploitation of human beings, leading to alienation and disenfranchisement for the poor.

For instance, Apple, famous for its iPhones and Mac computers, is known to have sweatshops in China despite its desire to project its public image as a benevolent corporate giant that makes its money and helps other parts of the world. When one turns to the hundreds of jobs Apple provides for people in China, one might argue that this capitalist giant helps provide employment for an otherwise unemployed underclass in China. However, the diabolic working conditions and wages at Apple sweatshops in China disrupt Apple's narrative as a gracious capitalist giant that provides economic benefits to others. In 2011, in less than six months, twelve employees of Foxconn, Apple's largest supplier in China, committed or attempted to commit suicide by jumping from buildings due to poisonous, inhumane working conditions. Their suicides shocked China and initiated discussions by US companies about corporate practices here and abroad. Many other examples abound in underdeveloped and developing countries, yet this dark side of capitalism is usually invisible to consumers. Nonetheless, people suffer.

This ahistorical assumption of capitalist history as progress must be questioned. Capitalist systems in America are generally interpreted as innately advantageous to the spreading of wealth and abundance: thus, "a rising tide raises all boats," an expression used by President Kennedy, and the "trickle-down economics" of President Reagan. Similarly, free-market logic is seen as an economic savior for underdeveloped, poverty-ridden countries. While market economies do provide measures of economic growth, laissez-faire logic (and its belief in the "invisible hand" of the market) complicates and underplays the profound importance of regulating structures to ensure an equitable distributions of wealth. The innate goodness and efficacy of American capitalism are simply questioned.

When critical questioning of advanced capitalism does occur, it usually disrupts this narrative of free-market logic and enables new visions of equality and equity to emerge, even within present capitalist arrangements. For instance, TOMS Shoes is a corporation that recognizes that all children do not have access to basic resources, such as shoes. In response to unfair conditions that the poor so often face, TOMS Shoes gives a free pair of shoes to disadvantaged persons around the world for every pair of shoes purchased. This company recognizes the profound importance of embracing visions of equity. There are also other economic models, such as socially conscious investing, that are questioning individualistic free-market logic and its deleterious effects on poor people. The next chapter provides a discussion of this point.

The theology of the current prosperity gospel movement has not turned a critical eye to capitalist production. Its singular focus on individual spirituality and action does not question the deep institutional patterns of inequality, social disrespect, and cultural degradation endured by the poor. Neither does this theology question its own assumptions about poverty (poverty represents an absence of faith in God) and how these assumptions abet and reinforce capitalist power. It simply calls upon individuals to do their part, showing no understanding of the extent to which both capitalism and poverty perpetuate themselves.

A NEW PROSPERITY GOSPEL?

This questioning of our capitalist moment is part of the intellectual activity within a particular type of church, which I will refer to as the *emerging Black Church*. The emerging Black Church is a church that is willing to be oriented to pursue a critical conversation about social issues, such as poverty, that affect the well-being of the disenfranchised. The emerging Black Church is characterized by its willingness to converse *across racial communities* about contestable socioeconomic issues rather than simply embracing an ethnic-specific (read: black) approach. The emerging Black Church is also committed to engage in dialogue about concepts of prosperity within religion and society rather than simply embracing or proclaiming a predigested, uncritical message of prosperity, as many church members and leaders have done in the past.

Within the emerging Black Church most agree that they are disillusioned with the institutional church as it is, because it often blindly supports many religious concepts. Instead, this new church believes that a radical orientation toward conversation and dialogue over these issues will strengthen their responses to the "least of these." The emerging Black Church is committed to strengthening its methods and strategies to secure thriving and abundance for all within its communities and the broader society. Black churches are able to fashion concepts of prosperity that do not collude with America's current materialistic consumer culture.

Turning Back for Images That Promote Hope

The questioning of goals and strategies to reach them can potentially lead to "dream images" that promote hope for the poor. "Dream images," a term used by Walter Benjamin, are the hopes and desires that offer freedom and flourishing to oppressed communities. Dream images are the "collective fantasy images deposited in the expressive qualities of daily life as well as in literature and art." They "arise from the secret communication between the oldest semantic potentials of human needs and the conditions of life generated by capitalism." Benjamin describes dream images as lodged in the collective unconscious mind that seek to transcend the "immaturity of the social product and the deficiencies of the social order of production."[14] They contain the seeds of protest against the death-dealing forces of advanced-capitalist arrangements and practices.

These dream images represent old promises lodged in the hearts of communities that have come and gone. As a result, oppressed communities cannot "turn to their liberated grandchildren for dream images; instead they must turn backward and critically remember and redeem the dream images lodged in the hearts and minds of their oppressed ancestors."[15] Progress is not necessarily achieved by moving history forward. Instead, redemption lies in turning to the past in order to see what the past "speaks" about, what it conveys and promises as a guide to human action. Retrieving such dream images is critically important in revealing new possibilities for liberation and flourishing.

Sociologist Zygmunt Bauman captures this turn backward toward the critical remembrance of dream images by using the metaphor of a graveyard. Bauman describes retrieving dream images from ancestral oppressed communities as a "graveyard" of possibilities. This metaphoric graveyard of possibilities entails

> coffins scattered all around the field; coffins precariously, never as neatly as one would wish, arranged in rows by the burial ground attendants called historians. Each coffin has a name attached, a singular name, but what it contains is a bundle of possibilities that has been murdered when the bearer of name died. The name belies the coffin's content: it speaks of death, not life, of fixation, not hope.[16]

This metaphor of a graveyard of possibilities discloses that these possibilities are not immortal. They are indeed vulnerable, and their extermination is easy. After experiencing the horrendous nightmare of the Holocaust, Benjamin knew that the "killing of hopes is the most common of human pastimes."[17] These hopes that reside in the past are often murdered with those who have died. Along with possibilities, hope is not immortal. Although it often dies with the bearer, it can be resurrected and redeemed when present generations turn to the past and revive these possibilities and hopes for their present.

Dream images of ancestors are often seen as the "trash of history," small pieces of "historical remembrance dismissed as insignificant, not deserving of attention, and unobtainable."[18] Yet, such "trash" of history can be rescued from the "history" that assigned it to oblivion. Such historical images can reveal the exploitation of people for profit as a history of catastrophe and allow an alternative history to break through. This alternative history is "a history of unfulfilled wishes for a life free of violence, injustice, and want." These dream images are often "stored in a society's material culture—in its commodities, institutions of consumption and distraction, and its popular literature."[19] They can be redeemed, whether through daily experiences, art, or texts.

These dream images or possibilities can only "come to life posthumously, in the act of resurrection." Through the development of a counternarrative, these lost or murdered possibilities can be exhumed and resurrected, fanning "the spark of hope in the past" as victories are chronicled.[20] The past *is* the true abode of future possibilities.

Benjamin notes that the Torah and its prayers are instructions in remembrance. In Judaism, remembrance is important in uncovering possibilities and hope within oppressive realities. He envisioned a particular kind of revolution within capitalist societies, a revolution that "gazes backward toward the ancestors."[21] For Benjamin, in order to respond faithfully to the "state of emergency" in the present—that of exploitative capitalism—we must look backward to the dream images and promises possessed by the ancestors. Thus, within the whirlwind of history that we call progress, the eyes of the *Angelus Novus* reflect the shock and horror at what is seen: chronic poverty, careless cruelty, and gross exploitation.

The Relation between Images and Hope

Images are important because knowledge often occurs as a succession of images within a culture. In our media-saturated daily lives, images "repeatedly hit us between the eyes."[22] Images that possess no predetermined meanings might provide spaces for exploring experience and finding illumination within social contexts. Images also entail a mass of contradictions that often accompany experience and meaning within cultural life. An image can "recreate the complexity of the world without suppressing one thought by another, without exerting conceptual violence."[23]

This turn back toward the ancestors is a central way in which womanist theology and ethics conceptualize the possibility of hope. As Monica Coleman states, "As we live into the present and future, our experiences become part of 'the past.' The past is available to be incorporated into the ongoing processes of life."[24] Womanist theologians continue to emphasize the role of memory and remembrance of ancestral communities in concepts of salvation and redemption. Theologian and ethicists such as Karen Baker-Fletcher, Emilie Townes, and Katie Cannon look to the ancestors (a few well-known names are Fannie Lou Hamer, Septima Clark, Ida B. Wells-Barnett, Sojourner Truth, and Harriet Tubman, among many others) to articulate how the past can be incorporated into our present efforts to achieve justice and flourishing.[25]

The redemption of dream images functions in much the same way—it enables us to theorize hope, grappling with the meanings and conditions that ground its possibility. The struggle of the ancestors was long and difficult, but they continued to move forward in hope. Learning about what has already been morally imagined in the hearts of "those who have despaired and suffered in the past" is essential to interpreting the reality of the present with a spirit of hope.

The redemption of dream images is critically important to hope itself. Hope can die; it is not immortal. It can be murdered, but it can also be resurrected. For the most part, the work of womanists has been the primary discourse in focusing on how black women experience hope. Such womanist discourse has emphasized the capacity of black women to act as agents in working to debunk that dominant social narratives that have diminished the worth of black women. There is concern, however, that such discourse has also downplayed the real despair that has gripped and choked the confidence, esteem, and life out of many poor black women. Many poor black women today feel robbed of agency and experience despair.

While poor black women have acted as moral agents and have "made ways out of no way" despite their impoverished conditions, the real disappointment and hopelessness that exists among poor black women must be acknowledged. However, deep feelings of dread, despair, and hopelessness often result from the social alienation poor black women experience within today's culture and economy. Denigrating cultural images and representations painfully affect the economic and educational opportunities open to many poor black women.

Black cultural critic bell hooks speaks about this "crisis of spirit" that ravages poor black communities. Her moving observations are worth quoting at length:

Every now and then I return to poor black communities I lived in or visited during my childhood. These neighborhoods that were once vibrant, full of life, with flowers planted outside the walls of run-down shacks, folks on the porch, are not barren landscapes. Many of them look like war zones. Returning, I bear witness to desolation. Surrounded by an aura of emptiness, these places, once shrouded in hope, now stand like barren arms, lonely and empty. No one moves into their embrace to touch, to be held and to hold, to comfort. Poverty has not created this desolation; the generations of folks who inhabited these landscapes have always been poor. What I witness are ravages of the spirit, the debris left after emotional assault and explosion. What I witness is heart-wrenching loss, despair, and a lovelessness so profound it alters the nature of environments both inside and out.

. . . More often than not this crisis of spirit is talked about by political leaders and community organizers as engendered by life-threatening poverty, violence or the ravages of addiction. While it is utterly true that all these forces undermine our capacity to be well, underlying these issues is a profound spiritual crisis. As a people we are losing heart. Our collective crisis is as much an emotional one as a material one. It cannot be healed simply by money.[26]

Hooks rightly describes poor black communities as wounded communities that do not experience respect, care, and dignity. Such wounding demonstrates how inequitable economic practices affect the culture, personality, and spirituality of the poor.

For instance, when the image of the black welfare queen is used in discussions of poverty and policy, it seeks to buttress and legitimate an economic logic that blames black women for their impoverished status. If economic success is due solely to people's motivation, hard work, and diligence, then the economic failures of poor black women are interpreted as their personal moral failures in being unwilling to participate in behaviors that ensure economic success. These images create fear in the minds of the American upper and middle classes, who see poor black women as indolent, leeching on the system in order to demand benefits from hardworking, responsible citizens. And these images create fear in the minds of the poor black women, who must bear the stigmatization in their struggle to survive in the face of an absence of opportunities for themselves and their children. In the end they perpetuate a certain culture of fear connected to the economic model of life in America.

It is important to examine how economic evils affect human personality and culture among the poor. For example, Korina (an inner-city, black, female resident) is given an opportunity for job training. She has experienced severe educational disadvantages and an absence of opportunities. When she is presented with job training, given her disappointing past experiences, how will she benefit from this single opportunity granted by what she knows to be an uncompassionate system? How will her disbelief in the system and its structures affect her performance on the job? These questions get at the heart of what hooks refers to as a crisis of spirit. Money and material resources are not all that is needed for well-being. Black women need a renewed sense of hope and confidence in America as a land that has opportunities *for them.* They must believe that America is a place that welcomes their self-actualization. In order to succeed, Korina needs this hope. She needs to believe that she will have a better future. The force of hope within the American political economy is critical.

The Black Churches and Hope

By fostering an economy of hope for poor black women, black churches can remember and redeem the dream image expressed in the Black Church–led Poor People's Campaign. I suggest that black churches can resurrect and redeem the PPC movement by promoting the image of *prosperity as the interplay between individual fulfillment and communal thriving.* This dream image includes an expanded concept of prosperity to temper and balance individual fulfillment with communal well-being.

Individual fulfillment at its best is each person's interests, desires, and longings being met and fulfilled *within* the web of relationships that sustain each individual. Practical theologian Dale Andrews notes that individual fulfillment means something quite different from individualism or self-interest. Individualism disrupts communal solidarity and responsibility in the pursuit of self-interests.[27] The opportunity and enhancement of the individual should be one goal of communal action and responsibility. However, the individual is situated within a broader community, and communal needs are as important as individual desires. Korina could find hope in such an image.

Individual fulfillment and communal well-being are thus inextricably related. They mutually inform and reinforce each other. The community flourishes as all individuals are able to grow and develop their potential. Conversely, as individuals experience fulfillment and actualize their potential, they are better positioned to contribute to goals related to communal flourishing. The individual and the community should not be in opposition. Arguments about prosperity as either individual success or communal flourishing are polarizing. Instead, the individual and the communal must work together if prosperity is going to be realized for all people.

Some black churches today are providing ministries that are attentive to both individual fulfillment and communal well-being; one such is the City of Refuge Church in San Francisco. Pastored by Bishop Yvette Flunder, this ministry provides social justice missions addressing structural issues of poverty and also provides programs geared toward individual flourishing, including spaces for same-gender-loving persons to self-actualize. Described as a ministry of radical inclusivity, the City of Refuge challenges the ways in which LGBTQ persons are often excluded from black church communities and broader society. By affirming practices that bring everyone to God's table regardless of race, ethnicity, class, nationality, and gender/sexuality, this church offers a word of hope to people by promoting a more loving, compassionate theology. City of Refuge provides a constant reminder that individual fulfillment and communal well-being are equally important.

The more dynamic concept of prosperity as the interplay between individual abundance and communal well-being critiques the prosperity gospel's narrow understanding of prosperity as the individual acquisition of material resources. This more critical understanding of prosperity gives black churches a language to counter the rabid, self-centered individualism of the American political economy. This expanded notion of prosperity directly affects how poverty is conceptualized and understood. Poverty is not seen as a curse or the result of an absence of faith. Instead, poverty is treated as a product of unequal economic arrangements and unfair access to resources.

The Benefits of Equitable Access to Resources

Wealth and socioeconomic well-being should be understood as something to be *shared* so that all might thrive. Within the Poor People's Campaign, Resurrection City gave each poor person a piece of land on which to build a home and thus own private property. A school and healthcare facility were built to provide quality access to health and education for all in the city. Although the educational and healthcare facilities posed a number of problems in terms of structural quality and sustainability, Resurrection City sought to bring forward a particular view of wealth and poverty. Wealth and poverty are profoundly connected to the economic arrangements in any society as well as to equity in accessing resources. Any maldistribution of resources contributes to deepening cycles of poverty among the poor, privileging the elites who continue to amass financial assets and capital at the expense of the poor.

Inequitable economic arrangements make it difficult and often impossible for the poor to rise out of poverty. The cadre of black churches that led the PPC realized that America's concept of wealth was lacking; it needed to expand to include everyone, both the rich and the poor. These black churches recognized that the poorest members within our American community were excluded from the broader society. Reducing inequalities helps not only the poor but also the wealthy. Wealth must be *shared* to improve society as a whole. This recognition of the importance of shared wealth contends that in order to be contributing members within their communities and larger society, the poor must be able to participate in the wealth-producing structures of society. Such norms of inclusion and participation in relation to wealth inform how true prosperity should be understood and practiced within churches and other social institutions.

Redeeming the narrative of the PPC and its expansive notion of wealth and prosperity can enable black churches to participate in a class-based vision of economic justice for all poor communities. The PPC and its dream image of prosperity as both individual fulfillment and communal well-being disrupt the narratives and ideas of standard prosperity gospel theology and its individualistic concepts of poverty and wealth. The Black Church can revive the hopeful possibilities of economic justice that its ancestors fought for. A moral consensus must be embraced once again in which prosperity and well-being are shared by all members within society.

Questioning our present capitalist moment and redeeming a more expanded concept of wealth and well-being can lead to a new kind of prosperity gospel. Such questioning exposes the real inadequacies in the way prosperity leaders link spirituality to narrow, individualistic notions of wealth. While there is much evidence of the relationship between positive thinking and heartfelt faith with mental, physical, relational, and spiritual well-being, it is mistaken to conclude that right thought or faith alone is sufficient. Even with faith, one will not necessarily succeed. Conversely, even if one lacks faith, one may become a high achiever. The prosperity gospel's linear approach neglects and/or underestimates the social nature of life in a given economic situation and physical environment. It is simply not true that individuals will succeed if they have enough faith.

The Black Church should advance a more compassionate prosperity gospel that (1) affirms the life-transforming power of faith, and (2) locates affirmative faith within the contexts of many factors, including environment, economics, relationships, and opportunity. Our well-being and suffering as persons are the result of many interdependent factors, including both God's lively vision for humanity and repressive social structures. Hence, individuals are not always fully responsible for their success, economic status, or educational level. A web of relationships forms and informs our journey toward success, wellness, and well-being. This web of relationships must also appropriate responsibility for failure. It is not always individuals who fail; more often it is a system that fails individuals.

A good example lies in our educational system. Poor black children are often at a distinct disadvantage within public school systems, especially those in inner cities or rural areas. These school systems are underfunded, poorly equipped, and inadequately staffed, affording these children a dearth of opportunities for academic advancement and growth. These children are victims within an educational system that is broken. How can they be solely responsible when they are unprepared to acquire adequate SAT and ACT scores that will get them admitted into a college? Even when these children want to advance, their faith alone does not secure their progress. Many children are unable to acquire the needed socioeconomic resources to rise out of these impoverished educational conditions. The vast majority of children are locked within a given educational system according to where they live.

A new understanding of prosperity can also address the distorted belief that faith is merely an individual decision; rather, faith emerges from experiences in relation to a faith tradition, family, communities, and more. Our ability to have faith or to hold positive images is not entirely our own doing—poverty, sexism, ageism, and homophobia (not to mention DNA, family of origin, and environmental degradation) can all limit our ability to be optimistic. These are important psychological and physiological considerations that are ignored by individually centered prosperity theologies.

Many people trapped in poverty, for example, experience physiological-based depression. Telling such persons that they continue to be depressed because they lack faith serves no useful purpose and undoubtedly would aggravate their depression. A new understanding of a prosperity gospel that links individual well-being with communal well-being will affirm and seek to understand these psychological and physiological factors as it discusses the ways in which the poor experience faith, hope, and well-being within fear-based, inequitable social arrangements.

While we are not entirely limited by our environment and can transform and transcend negative social scripts and experiences, black churches are ethically responsible for acknowledging the profound role socioeconomic and cultural environments play in either hindering vulnerable members from flourishing or in ensuring the success of such persons. Black religious institutions can aid the poor, particularly poor black women, within their own communities by creatively envisioning what type of just environments and social arrangements are possible within our American society. They can creatively articulate an economy of hope that fosters trust, social responsibility, and creativity so that the poor are empowered to experience well-being. They can encourage social responsibility and the creation of a social order that enables the poor and their children to dream dreams and see visions (see Joel 2:28). But they must not lose sight of the fact that the poor also need the social and relational resources to bring these dreams and visions to life. They must not ignore any real obstacles that frustrate a sense of well-being. They must cultivate both an economy of hope and a concept of thriving.

7

An Asset-Building Policy Approach

Today's black churches *can* fashion a new kind of prosperity gospel that cultivates inclusion and mutual participation so that the poor are able to develop their own human capabilities within America's present institutions. As the previous chapter noted, such a new approach would not only foster an economy of hope for poor black women but also cultivate a class-based concept of thriving in order for these women (as well as other poor groups) to secure the economic and sociocultural resources to flourish.

Within black theological and religious scholarship, scant attention has been paid to a concept of thriving for the poor, particularly poor blacks. And very little attention has been paid to the importance of public policies and strategies that foster equity and equality for the poor. Moreover, current black discourse on the poor tends to privilege income-focused strategies along with the need for social benefits such as healthcare and childcare. In other words, poverty (and the idea of thriving) seems to be framed exclusively in terms of insufficient income. There are certainly advantages to be gained; however, one assumption of an income-focused approach is that the surest way out of poverty is through increasing income and expanding benefits. This assumption is only partially adequate. What is needed is a broader concept of thriving that goes beyond income to include the building of financial and cultural assets.

Public policy related to poverty and thriving has seen a gradual shift in focus from an income-based paradigm to an asset-based paradigm. Any morally adequate response to poverty must be based on a multi-ethnic, class-based concept of thriving that includes complementary efforts aimed at enabling asset development among the poor. This chapter describes how institutional structures and public policies facilitate the accumulation of financial and other assets by the nonpoor and it also urges that similar supports be made available to the poor. Providing similar subsidies for the poor should render efforts to reduce poverty more equitable and more effective and sustainable, and in the long term should reduce poverty. To be certain, such an approach articulates a *long-term moral vision* about ways to reduce poverty by developing the capabilities of the poor so they can participate with their peers as contributing members of society. This class-based concept of thriving is guided by the norm of participatory parity; it privileges an asset-building approach to public policies intended to alleviate poverty and encourages socially conscious capitalism. Black churches can participate in advancing a discourse of thriving for poor persons by advocating for asset-building policy approaches.

THE NORM OF PARTICIPATORY PARITY

As a first step, and in order for flourishing to be a real possibility for the poor, the poor must be able to participate in society on a par with their nonpoor peers. Feminist theorist Nancy Fraser's work on a politics of redistribution, accompanied by a politics of social recognition, is important in addressing the question of thriving for the poor. While Fraser acknowledges the importance of social recognition in the face of injustices resulting from sexual, racial, and gender differences, she argues that the redistribution of resources is not only equally important but essential. She asserts that social justice today requires both redistribution and social recognition, and she devises a two-dimensional conception of social justice "that can accommodate both defensible claims for social equality [in the economy] and defensible claims for recognition of difference."[1] Fraser refers to this two-dimensional conception of justice as *participatory parity*, which enables all persons to participate equally with one another, assuming respect of differences.

Her norm encompasses both an objective condition and what she terms an "inter-subjective" condition. The inter-subjective condition (a politics of social recognition) "ensures that the institutionalized patterns of cultural value express equal respect for all participants and ensure equal opportunity for achieving social esteem." It precludes institutionalized norms and cultural values that systematically depreciate some categories of people or qualities associated with them that subordinate or impede their flourishing and thriving.[2] This recognizes that cultural norms can impede the parity of participation for some groups whose difference is characterized as socially "deviant."

The objective condition (a politics of redistribution) "precludes forms and levels of economic dependence and inequality that impede parity of participation." Moreover, "precluded are social arrangements and institutionalized deprivation, exploitation, gross disparities of wealth and income . . . thereby denying some people the means and opportunities to interact with other peers."[3] Fraser submits that the inter-subjective and objective dimensions of this overarching norm articulate a *single integrated, ethical framework for social justice* in relation to the poor and marginalized.

This idea of parity recognizes that social justice involves a singular approach and principle that integrates both a politics of social recognition and a politics of redistribution. For her, this two-dimensional concept of justice is irreducible to one or the other. These two conditions reflect the two-dimensional conception of parity that attempts to ensure that the symbolic/cultural *and* material aspects of injustices are equally addressed.[4] In addition, Fraser notes that discursive, democratic procedures are the best way to deal with issues of recognition and redistribution. Hence, Fraser argues that "the norm of participatory parity can be applied dialogically and discursively, through democratic processes of public debate."[5]

Because the poor do not presently experience participatory parity, they are limited in ~~what they can do and be~~ within America. For instance, poor black women suffer from a lack of cultural resources due to the social stigmatization they continue to experience. Their lack of social recognition leads to their political marginalization, which in turn vitiates their ability to participate in decision-making structures. They also experience a structural absence of economic and employment opportunities, which leads to material deprivation and poverty. In the end, poor black women simply do not have the inter-subjective and objective conditions to participate on a par with other groups and individuals within American society. This lack of parity deeply affects their confidence and esteem as members of the society. Fraser's norm recognizes the cultural disrespect and economic inequities that thwart poor black women's prospects for thriving and commits to addressing the oppressive aspects of both culture and economy in relation to their well-being.

A Model of Deliberative Democracy

While this norm is helpful in understanding the moral significance of economy (redistribution) and culture (social recognition), it does not substantively nuance problems of hegemony in relation to social recognition and issues of difference. For example, democratic electorates could grant poor black women basic material needs through social welfare programs but still not strengthen the participatory structures that recognize and honor these women's identities and differences. It is important to recognize that issues of "mis-recognition" of difference and authority complicate democratic participation, which inevitably affects policymaking. Power relations that assign particular values to differences often hamper the achievement of social recognition within democratic, deliberative spaces.

A deliberative democracy involves both dominant and marginalized groups who are constituted by particular histories and narratives. Difference can take many forms—identity politics, otherness, diversity, pluralism, and struggles for recognition—and each of these intertwined concepts complicates democratic principles such as equal respect and equal opportunity. Consequently, social recognition of difference is in need of a model of democracy that unravels the real power interests that make social recognition difficult.

Feminist critical theorist Seyla Benhabib's model of deliberative democracy is helpful. Her concept of the "reversibility of perspectives" is fruitful in discussing the real power interests involved in social recognition. Her "reversibility of perspectives" is a model of deliberative democracy that encourages a moral conversation in which each participant is invited to listen deeply in order to understand the "concrete other." Benhabib describes the "concrete other" as a vision of self that is particular, specific, and different, which is contrasted to the "generalizable other." The generalizable other is a self that is "defined by right, autonomy, and agency, but is dis-embedded and dis-embodied."[6] The poor must be treated as "concrete others" within our deliberative decision-making spaces in order to respond to their experiences of deprivation.

Within any public sphere deep social complexities are associated with difference. A politics of social recognition that acknowledges the concrete other is key to taking seriously the sociopolitical challenges that power and authority pose to difference. Although I agree with Fraser that social recognition involves changing the valuing of cultural patterns and ideas that decrease participatory parity for marginalized groups, Fraser's notion of participatory parity does not clarify *how* this occurs. Benhabib is right that this process can begin only by acknowledging and engaging the concrete other. It must involve moral conversations and deep listening within deliberative spaces; Fraser's norm of participatory parity does not explicitly capture this need.

What is most important in this discussion of the norm of parity is that *increased income for the poor does not necessarily lead to participation among the poor within society, that is, to them being seen as concrete others.* What is required is a long-term, sustainable approach and strategy guided by a concept of thriving. The poor must be able to participate on a par with their nonpoor peers, which means addressing both unfair cultural productions and inequitable economic structures that impede their participation in the economy and the wider culture. To thrive, the poor need to be able to participate in the development of their own human capabilities to flourish,[7] which means having the cultural and economic resources to participate within society in the same way as citizens with means.

The Problems of Identity Politics

The norm of parity challenges an identity-model approach to black women's poverty. Also known as identity politics, this approach reduces questions of economic justice to issues of cultural depreciation and demeaning cultural representations and practices. Thus, an approach based on identity politics would reduce class injustices among poor black women to cultural factors such as racism. While this model contains insights on the effects of racism, sexism, heterosexism, and cultural imperialism, it treats the poverty of black persons solely as a problem of cultural depreciation and demeaning cultural representations. But the recognition and acceptance of black women in terms of cultural respect will not remedy the economic inequities that poor black women experience. Identity politics by itself will fail at attempts at the equitable redistribution of opportunities and resources.[8]

While the identity-politics model acknowledges that cultural injustices are often inextricably linked to economic inequalities, it often "misunderstands the character of these links." Such a model would maintain that "economic inequalities are simple expressions of cultural hierarchies" in which "maldistribution can be remedied indirectly, by a politics of recognition" and that "to revalue unjustly devalued identities is simultaneously to attack deep sources of economic inequality."[9] As a consequence, this identity model does not explicitly foreground the need for a politics of redistribution. The politics of social recognition displaces any politics of redistribution, eliminating any possibility of economic justice.

Unfortunately, markets within our system of advanced capitalism follow a logic of their own; they are neither wholly constrained by cultural patterns nor subordinate to them. Markets generate their own economic disparities and inequalities. The shift from an industrial economy to a post-industrial economy described in Chapter 3 and the associated economic miseries result from economic variables within labor markets and from economic structures that cannot be reduced to cultural hierarchies and valuations. America's post-industrial society has generated an underclass in which poor rural whites and poor urban Hispanics are as deeply affected as poor black women. An identity-model approach to social recognition is simply not sufficient.

An associated problem is that stressing the need to generate a healthy, affirming collective identity puts pressure on individual members to conform to a certain group culture. Fraser notes that the overall effect is "to impose a single, drastically simplified group-identity which denies the complexity of people's lives, the multiplicity of their identifications and the cross-pulls of their various affiliations."[10] As a result, the identity model approach can actually render struggles invisible *within* a group, struggles for power and the authority to represent.[11]

Because struggles within a group are hidden from view, this model often reinforces and exacerbates intra-group domination and repressive forms of intolerance. As argued earlier, racism alone is not responsible for the economic miseries of poor black women, and poor black women's opportunities do not necessarily reflect the opportunities or cultural experiences of middle- to upper-class black women. These are several reasons why an identity-politics approach to public policy for poor black women is inadequate.

The goal is to conceptualize struggles for social recognition as distinct from yet interrelated to struggles for redistribution. I find Fraser helpful in articulating the relationship and moral significance between social recognition and redistribution in order to explore the conditions toward the possibility of thriving for poor black women. These women need both positive cultural valuation *and* relief from mal-distribution. Participatory parity becomes essential. Such a two-dimensional conception of justice makes room for defensible claims for economic equality *and* recognition of difference. The poor need to experience participatory parity, in which each person possesses the cultural, economic, and social resources to participate on a par with his or her nonpoor peers.

ARE INCOME-BASED PARADIGMS ENOUGH?

While anti-poverty reduction strategies have focused on meeting the poor's needs, they have not necessarily granted them the economic resources to participate on a par with their nonpoor peers. Focusing on meeting the immediate needs of the poor is legitimate and important; however, it is often the primary and/or singular response to poverty. Since poverty is understood as having insufficient income to meet the basic needs, the goal of anti-poverty policies has been dominated by policy efforts to raise the income (or purchasing power) of the poor. The aim of these policies is to provide just enough financial aid to allow poor persons to consume at a level that will raise them out of poverty. As discussed earlier, the welfare reform debate focused on how to provide incentives for women to work, how to move them beyond their monthly expectation of receiving cash payments.

Earlier, I outlined some basic assumptions that undergird this policy, including the primary one that suggests that poverty would be reduced if public policies stopped encouraging dependency on the government. Yet, numerous studies show that welfare mothers who work still endure debilitating circumstances such as low wages. In addition, their work benefits do not typically include sick leave, childcare, employer-sponsored health insurance, and so forth. Being employed in no way secures a life free from poverty for these women.

There is a second assumption that grounds current anti-poverty legislation. This is a *liberal* assumption, an assumption that poverty can be adequately addressed, if not eliminated, through cash payments and time-limited benefits (government income transfers). James Bailey notes:

A great deal of evidence can be extracted in favor of this liberal approach. Income transfers do significantly raise the income of the poor and ease their burdens, increasing the number of persons living above poverty line. Clearly, governmental transfers do substantially increase the levels of income for many poor Americans and reduce the hardship associated with poverty. At the same time, there is mounting evidence over the last decade that suggests that such income-based approaches are inadequate. While income transfers are effective in addressing the *symptoms* of poverty, they seem to be less effective in altering the *underlying causes* of poverty.[12]

Even though the political right and left advocate for different approaches to the problem of poverty, they both articulate poverty as a deficiency of income. They describe poverty as the inability of families and persons to "secure a minimal level of consumption."[13] Hence, current policy solutions to remedy poverty focus almost exclusively on increasing the level of consumption so the poor can meet their basic needs.[14] "Thriving" is understood within public policy as increasing income and consumption levels for the poor through means-tested income transfers such as rental subsidies or food stamps. This overemphasis on income-based paradigms to alleviate poverty and/or bring about thriving is shared by conservatives and liberals.

There certainly is justification for this focus on income-based paradigms. Income is a necessity when poor families find themselves unable to meet their basic needs. Surely thriving cannot be approached when poor persons are trying to survive. Moreover, this emphasis on income supplements the pitiful, unjust wages that many poor mothers receive. However, this *exclusive* focus on income to ameliorate poverty should be challenged. The issue is not whether income is important. It clearly is. The issue is whether income (such as cash payments and food stamps) is sufficient to give the poor the necessary financial resources to escape cycles of poverty. Surviving is not the same thing as thriving. In addition to income, the poor need access to economic and cultural resources in order to participate on a par with their contemporaries who are not poor. We need policies that allow the poor to participate equally and to accumulate assets that will keep them from slipping back into poverty. Unless anti-poverty initiatives *integrate some long-term vision of asset building, efforts to ameliorate poverty will not be successful.*

The Need to Build Assets

Treating asset building as a paradigm suggests that an asset-building approach marks a significant shift away from income-focused legislation.

Most income-based approaches to poverty reduction are nothing more than "stopgap measures to help people through financial crisis brought on by loss of work, unexpected illness, the death of a wage earner, and so on."[15] But poverty remains a persistent, intergenerational problem because the poor are unable to establish a secure financial future that will keep them out of poverty. I maintain that an asset-building approach (supported by a clear, practical strategy) can offer a more sustainable plan for poverty reduction.

For example, let's think about the financial future of two companies: Strategic Alliance and Flawless Cuts. Strategic Alliance has assets, while Flawless Cuts has been unable to develop assets. Suddenly, the economy experiences a serious recession. Because Strategic Alliance has assets, it is clearly in a better position to avoid financial disaster during the recession. In fact, Strategic Alliance has more of a competitive advantage in the marketplace than Flawless Cuts because it can leverage its assets to maintain employee morale and its level of productivity. Unfortunately, Flawless Cuts struggles to survive in the marketplace. Flawless Cuts might have to lay off employees, which could compromise organizational productivity and morale. If Flawless Cuts needs a loan, it would be very hard (if not impossible) to obtain; if it did receive a loan, it would come with very high interest. While Strategic Alliance's financial situation would probably enable it to survive the recession, Flawless Cuts' financial future is precarious and uncertain.

This example illustrates quite clearly why income-based strategies alone are insufficient in fashioning a long-term approach to economic well-being. Income and assets play distinctly different roles in providing a solid financial future. If the poor are to have a secure financial future, they must be empowered to participate in asset building.

Numerous studies also cite the psycho-social effects and benefits associated with having assets. Edward Scanlon and Deborah Page-Adams have concluded that there is growing evidence that assets

> are associated with economic household stability; decrease economic strain on households; are associated with educational attainment; decrease marital dissolution; decrease the risk of intergenerational poverty transmission; increase health and satisfaction among adults; decrease residential mobility; increase property maintenance; and increase local civic involvement.[16]

Michael Sherraden, a professor of social development, adds that "assets permit long-term thinking and planning, provide a foundation for taking risk, increase personal efficacy and sense of well-being, lead to greater development of human capital, increase social status and social connect the well-being and life-chances of offspring."[17]

Households without assets face greater uncertainty than those with assets. Like Flawless Cuts, when a reces pected incident occurs (such as illness or loss of a job), ..., sufficient assets is more likely to experience economic duress. This lack of a financial stability, in part, helps explain why welfare mothers move on and off welfare rolls. In the absence of asset ownership, any loss of income can be catastrophic, leaving the poor with no options other than government help or charitable aid. Such duress can overwhelm families and even entire communities with feelings of low morale and confidence about the future. Economic catastrophe impedes people's ability to imagine a secure future and adds to their sense of anxiety and fear. The poor often face such socioeconomic crises on a daily basis. It is reasonable to become disillusioned and discouraged about future possibilities when one sees no way to accumulate assets or raise one's income. Lacking assets, the poor live a difficult and precarious existence. A strategy to help them develop assets is needed if they are to thrive rather than simply survive.

A Lack of Assets: Whose Fault?

Some argue that the poor are at fault for their lack of assets. However, asset discrimination has a long history within America, particularly among ethnic groups such as African Americans and Native Americans. Many studies document the existence of a substantial wealth gap between white and black Americans that moves beyond differences in income.[18] This disparity between white and black wealth can be explained historically in large part by particular public policies that favor wealth-accumulation opportunities for whites and deny these same opportunities to African Americans. Public policies do have a significant impact on people's ability to accumulate wealth. Public policies have encouraged both asset discrimination and asset denial. While African Americans have experienced asset denial, other minority groups, such as Native Americans, have experienced asset discrimination through policy. Historically, African Americans have been adversely affected by two major public policies: the Homestead Act of 1862 and the Southern Homestead Act of 1866, dealing with land ownership; and the Great Depression–era initiatives intended to protect and promote property ownership. Moreover, the current use of restrictive covenants in housing and the practice of redlining, even though made illegal by 1968 legislation, continue this history of discrimination for many African Americans as well as other minority communities.

THE PROBLEMS OF ASSET DISCRIMINATION

Historically, racial injustice has had a severe impact on asset accumulation for African Americans. The first public policy with a direct impact on asset accumulation among African Americans was the Homestead Act of 1862, signed into law by Abraham Lincoln. This Act was one of the nation's first major domestic policies that included a significant asset-building measure after the Emancipation Proclamation.[19] This Act communicated the government's intention to distribute unoccupied government land to persons who were not landowners during the era of Reconstruction. Over the life of the Act, over "287.5 million acres of the public domain were granted or sold to homesteaders. This figure represents roughly ██ ████████ ███ ██████ █████ ██████ █████ ████████ ████s with few or no assets could "find an unoccupied 160 acres, file a homestead application, and after living on the land for five years, possess crops, land, and financial independence."[20] The government was not merely giving away land but providing an opportunity for upward mobility and a more secure future for families. Scholars widely acknowledge that the Homestead Act has shaped the settlement of land in the United States well into the twenty-first century.[21]

The Emancipation Proclamation (1863) and the Thirteenth Amendment (1868) freed some four million slaves, but the vast majority of former slaves, or "freedmen," did not own property or any other assets. Through the Homestead Act, Lincoln extended land ownership and asset rights to them. Former slaves were given land that had been confiscated during the Civil War (including land from some of their former slave masters) in order to begin the process of settling and farming the land. Lincoln knew that the freedom of former slaves and the freedom of their children could not be sustained without both income *and* land ownership (assets).[22] However, in the wake of Lincoln's assassination in 1865, his successor, Andrew Johnson, reversed these initial gains that attempted to "level the playing field" in relation to assets and land. Being more "sympathetic to Southern loyalties and interests," Johnson "extended amnesty to Southerners who had participated in the war and restored their property rights to land that newly freed slaves had already settled on."[23] Freedmen knew that President Johnson's actions in stripping them of their land encroached upon their new rights and freedoms.

Measures to Hinder Land Ownership

Appealing to Johnson through petitions, the freedmen argued that this action was an injustice, that they had "labored without pay for years and fought on behalf of the Union but were being stripped of their land in favor of those who had fought against the Union and enslaved them."[24] Not only the freedmen were incensed at Johnson's political maneuvers; congressional members were also outraged. In an effort to respond to Johnson's blatant actions of injustice, Congress acted swiftly and passed the Southern Homestead Act of 1866, which gave the freed slaves prospects of owning income-generating property.[25]

While the intent of the Act was to enable the distribution of land to whites and blacks alike, blacks continued to experience institutional discrimination. For example, whites were able to purchase land directly with the help of low-interest loans from banks. By contrast, blacks could acquire land only through a government agency known as the Freedmen's Bureau, which placed many restrictions on ownership of land for them. Bureau officials maintained that "newly freed slaves should not simply be gifted with land but rather should earn it."[26] It was recommended that Northerners (including Bureau agents) should purchase or lease farms to provide work for the freedmen. Not only did Northerners end up owning the greatest number of confiscated plantations, but "this measure also laid the groundwork for the sharecropper system that would return former slaves to systems of indentured servitude."[27] The Homestead Act of 1862 and the Southern Homestead Act of 1866 provided a context in which asset discrimination would flourish.

The Freedmen's Bureau was closely associated with the Freedmen's Savings and Trust Company, an institution created by Congress to assist blacks in creating wealth; most Southern banks refused to accept deposits from freedmen. Within five years of its founding, freedmen had deposited nearly "17 million dollars, and by July 1872, this savings had grown to over 31 million dollars." However, the bank declared bankruptcy and failed after accepting deposits from free blacks for almost a decade. The reason for the bank's failure further corroborates the diabolic discrimination that blacks endured. The "bank failed in 1874 mostly as a result of questionable no-interest loans from the bank to white companies, decisions made by the bank's all-white board of directors."[28]

The collapse of this bank left many blacks distrustful and deeply suspicious of American financial institutions. W. E. B. Du Bois remarked,

Then in one sad day came the crash,—all the hard-earned dollars of the freedmen disappeared; but that was the least of loss,—all the faith in saving went too, and much of the faith in men; and that was a loss that a Nation which to-day sneers at Negro shiftlessness has never yet made good.[29]

Obstacles Put in Place in the Twentieth Century

Asset building for blacks was not only impeded and limited by the Freedmen's Bureau, the banks, and the discrimination embedded in the Homestead Acts of the nineteenth century, but also was profoundly hindered by the initiatives of the New Deal Era. African Americans were constantly denied access to benefits associated with New Deal programs. One example is the most widely appreciated initiative of the New Deal, the Social Security Act of 1935. One part of this Act, the old-age assistance/insurance programs, offered millions of Americans some modest financial security during retirement.

However, this program "virtually excluded African Americans and Latinos from its benefits." Blacks and Latinos were effectively excluded because the program exempted "agricultural and domestic workers from coverage." African Americans, who were disproportionately represented in these job categories, were thus disproportionately excluded from the benefits of Social Security.[30] Blacks were simply locked out of a government program that offered modest retirement and financial security. These exclusions were seen as necessary by some Northern politicians to gain the political support of Southern congressmen.

Over the last few decades to the present, this historical legacy of asset discrimination and denial has persisted for African Americans, Latino/as, and other immigrant communities. For instance, in the 1960s, tactics at the local level, often sponsored by organized neighborhood associations to ensure that white neighborhoods remained white, accompanied the federal endorsement of integration.

These associations employed a divers set of strategies to achieve their goal, including advocating for zoning restrictions that prevented blacks from living in a particular neighborhood and threatening to boycott real estate agencies and companies that offered services and goods to blacks. They also threatened bodily harm to black homeowners who accepted an offer by white homeowners, as they did not want blacks living in their neighborhoods. They even fashioned "restrictive covenants," which were "contractual agreements among property owners stating that they would not permit a black to own, occupy, or lease their property."[31]

These covenants were "sanctioned by the courts, affirmed politically by real-estate boards, and rendered 'morally' permissible by real estate professional associations."[32] Although the effects of these covenants were numerous, the most significant one was that blacks were denied access to property—and property that was appreciating at a relatively rapid rate. Thus, throughout much of the end of the twentieth century, African Americans were instead confined to urban centers, where property lost value.[33]

Consequently, even today, blacks have not been able to benefit from the huge appreciation in home equity.

Asset Building Post–2008

As noted in Chapter 3, the sub-prime mortgage crisis of 2008 struck African Americans particularly hard because "they were specifically targeted by banks peddling dangerous sub-prime mortgages. When people applied for home mortgages, blacks were far more likely than whites to receive the high cost loans."[34] Those that suffer under the burden of sub-prime mortgage exploitation are often morally stigmatized and blamed by public officials; however, the fault lies much more with those who fashioned and created such loans rather than the people receiving the loans. This is not to say that recipients of these loans have no direct responsibility. However, their actions were easily overshadowed by the reckless, predatory behavior of financial elites who greedily pursued high rates of return without compunction. In addition, lawmakers, policymakers, and corporate executives encouraged these immoral actions. As has been widely concluded, the burden of failure rests on the financial industry and governmental institutions that did nothing to curb such predatory behavior.

Every major economic collapse over the last 125 years has been provoked by some kind of excess in the banking and financial industry. In every case the most vulnerable in society, particularly African Americans, have suffered disproportionately for the failings of this industry. And, it must be recognized that this history of asset denial and wealth discrimination has been *a matter of public policy*. Public policy remedies have either ignored or failed to recognize the degree to which institutional discrimination (such as race and now class) has played a role in the financial difficulties of the poor.

This history of asset discrimination and denial has had a profound and alarming effect on the financial security of many African Americans. At the time of the Emancipation Proclamation, "blacks owned 0.5 percent of the total wealth in this country. By 1990, the wealth of black Americans had risen to a meager 1 percent of the total wealth."[35] These statistics in part are the legacy of a history of public policy that has disenfranchised blacks, denying them opportunities to build assets that would provide for a more secure financial future.

While racial discrimination continues to persist, recently class exclusion has become more pronounced. Class exclusion from the benefits of asset-building policies is a current problem because "many of the benefits of these policies are delivered through the federal income tax code as well as other financial vehicles that provide incentives for the nonpoor to invest and save."[36] (Think, for example, of the reduced tax rate on capital gains and the benefits of owning a tax-exempt Roth IRA.) While asset-building policies and vehicles have proliferated in recent years, the benefits have been largely directed toward middle- and upper-class communities. Those who do not earn enough to pay federal income taxes do not benefit from these policies. In other words, current public policy actually exacerbates wealth inequality.

ASSET-BUILDING POLICIES FOR THE POOR

Since most impoverished people earn so little that they do not have to pay federal taxes, they do not benefit from the same incentives and rewards that are built into current asset-building policies. Many middle- and upper-class persons who have been able to take advantage of these policies have been very successful at building moderate wealth. Could public policies designed to provide the poor with benefits similar to those that are currently given to the nonpoor be successful? Could public subsidies be used to help structure, stimulate, and contribute to savings for the poor, as they do for the nonpoor? These are important questions because the poor are often seen as unable or unmotivated to save. Some argue that the poor might not be poor if they had made different choices. Consequently, some conclude that no amount of government intervention will change the conditions of those who experience deprivation. To rise out of poverty, the poor must make a choice to forsake the habits and ways that led them into cycles of poverty.

This question about the ability of the poor to save should be seen within a larger context. The decisions that are made by the nonpoor to save occur within a broader institutional context that rewards saving and investing. Recent research suggests that the framing of decisions to save can determine saving and investing behavior. For example, there is some disparity in participation rates in 401(k) plans when workers are required to opt into the plan versus when employees are required to opt out of the plan.[37] In one study of workers who were automatically signed up for such a plan but allowed to opt out if they so chose, "90 percent of the workers participated immediately and more than 98 percent within thirty-six months."[38]

Behavioral economist Ray Boshara contends that public policies should be crafted to make "savings and asset accumulation automatic by getting everyone into savings systems at four critical time periods: at birth, at one's place of employment, at tax time, and at the time when Americans pursue their major asset, their home."[39] However, even when these structures are present, in an economy that continues to suffer from high unemployment, inflation, and slow growth, even the nonpoor find it difficult to save.[40] This institutional context is extremely important.

Individual Development Accounts

Would the ability of the poor to save be enhanced if they had access to institutional incentives that encouraged and rewarded them for saving and investing? This question has been explored, and a government program has been created that actually demonstrates that the poor can save when they have access to institutions and incentives that reward their savings, as do the nonpoor. Known as Individual Developmental Accounts (IDAs), these accounts are similar to IRAs. Mark Schreiner and Michael Sherraden assert:

> Just as IRAs are subsidies by the government through tax exemptions, IDAs are subsidized either through the government (in the form of direct expenditures) or by non-profit organizations. Money deposited into an IDA account is matched according to a predetermined formula. In order to receive matching funds, the IDA account holder must spend the money according to pre-defined categories. "Matched-withdrawals" are those that are spent on asset-building endeavors such as homeownership, a college education, or ownership of a small business. IDA account holders are required to attend financial classes that range from financial planning to managing debt.[41]

Today, between five hundred and one thousand programs exist in about thirty states that include IDAs as part of their welfare reform plans.[42] Such states have passed some form of IDA legislation. The data collected on IDA programs affirms that the poor can and do save if they have access to the same institutional mechanisms as the nonpoor. IDA legislation must be integrated into the policy frameworks of more states in order to build further upon these efforts.

There are direct psychological benefits associated with individuals who are IDA account holders. Ninety-three percent of IDA account holders reported that they "felt more confident about the future" and attributed it to the IDA program. "Eighty-four percent reported that they felt more economically secure, and 85 percent felt they were in control of their lives." Such programs have been shown to "have positive effects on expectations and confidence about the future as well as inducing more prudent personal behavior."[43]

IDA programs represent a paradigm shift in poverty alleviation. This paradigm shift argues that an increase in income alone is not a sufficient answer to poverty. While income supports, greater opportunities for work, and higher wages are central to poverty reduction, they must be supplemented with asset-building policies, including IDAs and other policy innovations such as Child Savings Accounts (CSA) and Child Trust Funds (CTF), which may help promote a culture of savings and give persons within cycles of deprivation a good start from birth. A national long-term commitment to such policy initiatives could enable this country to address and perhaps remedy some of its asset inequalities. *Such programs could alter inequities and diminish the intergenerational transmission of poverty.*

Asset-Building vs. Market Logic

There are, however, limitations and dangers in relation to asset-building policies (such as IDAs) among the poor. Asset-building policies do not really address the basic problematic nature of capitalist systems and regimes that are radically consumerist and are sustained by the exploitation of many to sustain the wealth of the few. If our capitalist regime is "unredeemable," these policies may do no more than help the poor to participate in a "minimal" way. Are our capitalist markets intrinsically designed to ensure the failure of the poor? Is exploitative market logic so inherent to capitalist economies that the poor cannot thrive within these existing arrangements? If the answer is yes to these questions, then asset building may not be desirable or sustainable.

Some critics of asset-building policies also worry that adopting policies such as IDAs would erode public and political support for income-based poverty policies. Some worry that this focus could undermine existing welfare provisions and needed financial aid. If the impoverished are not able to develop their income and wage capacity, asset building will not be possible. These critics maintain that in the beginning, policy must focus on securing income and wage increases for the poor before attempting to craft asset-building measures. Hence, while these critics do not reject asset-building policies in principle, they argue that it is not politically wise to rely on such a policy shift without adequate measures to ensure sustainable income supports.[44]

These two concerns—the basic nature of our present capitalist system and the fear of losing income-supplanting policies—are legitimate. As noted earlier, I do not believe that capitalism, socialism, or any other economic system is particularly virtuous or evil in itself. The question is not whether our present economic system needs to be replaced by a "better" or "more equitable" one. Rather, the issue seems to be whether the benefits of any economic system are distributed in such a way that all persons can thrive. The American market economy generates a tremendous amount of wealth; however, this wealth has not been distributed in ways that are equitable. The poor, in particular, are exploited and left out of wealth-producing structures. We have a capitalist system that needs to exploit their labor and social class. It seems that the real question is how the poor can survive, or thrive, within existing arrangements that *could* share the wealth being produced *but choose not to?*

In order to address the second concern—that asset-building policies would supplant income-based policies—it is important to situate asset-building initiatives within a larger moral framework. The paradigm shift toward asset building introduces a moral vision for policy in which *the poor are active and contributing members of society instead of being seen solely in light of their needs.* Current poverty policies tend to construct the poor as objects of charity who are not able to contribute to human communities. Defining the poor other than by their needs embraces a vision of human worth and dignity grounded in the poor's participation within the life of the broader society. This moral vision articulates the importance of a social reality in which all persons share through their participation. The norm of participation as central to what it means to be "human" is critical to thriving for persons experiencing poverty.

This moral vision also makes a distinction between the nonpoor creating a relief economy for the poor versus the poor and nonpoor as co-creators of a sustainable economy in which all participate equally so that all flourish. A singular focus on income means that the poor receive only financial relief. Financial relief does not necessarily lead to flourishing, nor is it sustainable. The poor deserve more. Asset-building policies, however, do include a deeper moral vision about how society is organized over time and how persons participate in creating and maintaining their own flourishing.

The Possibilities of Socially Conscious Capitalism

While I primarily advocate a class-based approach in addressing black women's poverty, it is important to recognize that advanced capitalist structures can also be challenged by the model of *socially conscious* capitalism. Many middle- and upper-class communities do not perceive a responsibility toward the poor because our society tends to worship such capitalistic values as individual merit, hard work, and achievement. Thus, corporate managers can perpetuate the exploitation of the poor without feelings of guilt or shame. Current business practices are usually justified and driven by a profit motive. However, *socially conscious capitalism* does exist and it has a role to play in strengthening the economic and political resources of poor communities, including employment opportunities, career training, and more. Socially conscious capitalism moves from a business model focused solely on the pursuit of profits to one focused on integrity, higher standards, and serving the interests of *all* stakeholders—investors, employers, employees, the community, and the world at large. Socially conscious capitalism assumes that the fundamentals of capitalism must change if entire communities are going to thrive.

Socially conscious capitalism comes from the more well-known term *conscious capitalism.* Coined by Muhammad Yunus, conscious capitalism was defined and implemented through the creation of the Grameen Bank in the late 1970s. The bank established credit delivery systems in order to give small loans to the rural poor in Bangladesh so they could create businesses. The business philosophy that undergirded Grameen Bank was that when the poor are able to obtain small loans without exploitative terms, they are able to reverse the "low income, low saving, and low investment" cycle to a "low income, opportunity for credit, investment, more income, more savings, more investment, more income" cycle.[45] Under the direction of Yunus, the Grameen Bank has served rural areas of Bangladesh and met with startling success, proving that the poor can be financially responsible when given institutional mechanisms that support their sense of thriving. In fact, this bank is owned by the rural poor that it serves; borrowers of the bank own 90 percent of its shares, while the government owns 10 percent.[46]

The conscious-capitalism model has two essential ingredients: conscious leadership and conscious business practices. To be a conscious corporate leader means to be awake to the ways in which one's leadership affects multiple constituencies. A conscious leader is authentic and aware of the implications of decisions, which also means maintaining an ongoing commitment to learning and personal growth.[47] Conscious leaders adopt a holistic worldview that sees their enterprises as part of a complex, interdependent, and evolving system with multiple constituencies. Conscious leaders see that profit is one of the important purposes of the business, but not the *sole* purpose. Most important, they reject a zero-sum trade-off view of business and "look for creative synergistic win-win approaches that offer multiple kinds of value simultaneously to all stakeholders."[48] In other words, conscious leaders begin with a positive vision of humanity and allow that vision to inform market decisions rather than allowing market forces alone to determine human relationships. Human values of care, trust, and compassion inform business culture and practices within the framework of conscious capitalism.

Thus, conscious capitalism is aware of its power to create a world that works for *all* by promoting the development of a system within which profitability increasingly contributes to human prosperity and environmental sustainability. Socially conscious capitalism suggests that both private capital and public policies within a society can be used to promote the public good, a community that is grounded in social trust, compassion, and participation in communal life. For poor black women, socially conscious capitalism can not only promote government aid through asset-building policies but also reinforce a very long tradition of communal help using private capital within communities to benefit "the least of these."

There is growing interest among corporations, businesses, organizations, and individuals in socially conscious capitalism. For example, Bentley University in Waltham, Massachusetts, has established the Conscious Capitalism Institute, which sponsors an annual conference. The institute's website states, "The Conscious Capitalism movement is fast gaining recognition and attracting adherents all around the world. Now more than ever, we need to rethink the fundamental precepts of how we conceptualize, run and teach about business and its impact on the world." And there are a number of forums around the world that are beginning to dedicate significant time, energy, and resources to challenging how capitalism is understood and practiced. These corporate leaders want to highlight a new model that resonates with communal flourishing for all members within our society.

There are also socially conscious businesses in America. For instance, Stonyfield Farm, a company that specializes in organic foods such as yogurt and milk, offers a Profits for the Planet grant program; the company gives 10 percent of its annual profits to efforts that help to protect and restore the earth. In the past Stonyfield Farm has awarded grants to PCC Farmland Trust, an organization that is not only dedicated to securing and preserving threatened farmland in the Pacific Northwest, but also to supporting local communities by employing farmers who will use the land to produce organic food. Thanks to Stonyfield Farms, the PCC Farmland Trust was able to preserve over one hundred acres of farmland in Pierce County, Washington. Ben & Jerry's also has tightened its commitment to be socially conscious and profitable by working with family farms and promoting environmental justice.

Black religious institutions should increase their efforts in being a part of these conversations on socially conscious capitalism in order to understand what role they can play in transforming the economy for the poor. Black religious institutions such as black churches must decide to integrate themselves into the fabric of those particular discussions. Black churches should also determine how private capital within black communities can be employed to help the long-term growth of the poor. Black communities, which have a long tradition of self-help and communal uplifting, can also strategize on how black capital is being used and how it might benefit its poor members. By promoting socially conscious capitalism among black businesses and capitalists, black churches can develop a theology of holistic prosperity that considers the thriving of all members within society.

Epilogue

Building a Movement
to End Poverty

A revolution is under way. People are beginning to recognize that something is wrong. The gap of inequality is widening, and people are becoming tired. The latest census data shows that "a record number of Americans—nearly 1 in 2—have fallen into poverty or are scraping by on earnings that classify them as low income."[1] We are witnessing this restlessness with extreme disparities and deep inequities as we turn our attention to the Occupy Wall Street movement, which is protesting the ways in which wealth is inequitably created and maintained. The poor (working and underclass populations) are just as much a part of this movement as intellectuals, professors, and other white-collar workers. Moreover, projects for the poor continue around the country to address the profound economic crisis we are presently experiencing. One project is the Poverty Initiative associated with Union Theological Seminary in New York, which brings religious communities together with the poor to fight poverty in its multiple manifestations. Simply put, we are witnessing the beginning of a revolution that I believe is going to have great implications for this century and beyond.

How are we, as a nation, going to respond to one of the greatest moral challenges of our time? We must ask ourselves what kind of America we want, not just today but fifty years from now. How will we get to this more equal and equitable America from one that is broken due to the disparities that are present between the rich and poor? Ending poverty is not just an economic challenge, but also a moral concern that will determine whether America is a place of thriving and flourishing for *all*, not just for some.

Black religious institutions such as black churches *must* help reframe and reshape our national debate on poverty, as blacks are disproportionately represented and experience unique forms of economic inequity due to racism. Yet, black religious and theological scholars (as well as black political and social leaders) must avoid articulating racial injustice as the singular, primary impetus for poverty among black women and men. Poor black women are part of a larger American underclass that goes across racial groups in which poor blacks, poor whites, poor Hispanics, and other minorities are affected by shifts in American political economy. Class injustice is increasingly significant for poor black women and a broader American underclass. While poor black women have more in common (in terms of economic opportunities) with poor Hispanics and poor rural whites than middle-class black women, poor black women do experience poverty in qualitatively different ways than poor rural whites or poor Latino/as. The *new* ways in which race, class, gender, and sexuality converge affect poor black women differently than other groups within an American underclass.

Consequently, black churches must reshape their anti-poverty strategies in ways that critique exploitative economic practices and structures. Black churches offer faith-based social services, which can certainly provide transcendence for such women, but they do not address the economic structures that maintain and exacerbate their cycles of impoverishment. Poverty is not about individual failings, an interpretation prominent within national discourse. Instead, poverty is largely reproduced through economic institutions and practices that have left an entire underclass population behind. This *institutional (re)production of deprivation* is what must be recentered within national discourse on poverty. Persons within religious communities such as black churches must make this connection between economic disparity and moral values. Economic disparity is not merely about personal irresponsibility. It is about inequitable economic institutions. Our moral values must change in relation to the economy. This book introduces a new set of moral values—compassion, social trust, social responsibility, participation, and thriving—that black churches can embrace to address poverty effectively within their own communities and to provide leadership to broader society concerning the amelioration and eradication of poverty across racial groups.

Black churches' leadership in poverty discourse can potentially ease some of the anxiety that surrounds religion's presence within politics. Religion is often seen as a destructive force or as oppositional to political and policy activism within a democratic order. However, religion and politics ought not be seen as anathema to each other. In particular, black churches have provided significant political and policy activism at specific moments in American history. As discussed, the Civil Rights movement, a quest for equality and opportunity for blacks, was initiated and largely led by a cadre of black churches committed to political freedom and justice within a supposedly democratic society that denied these very freedoms to black people. Similarly, black churches can reach back into this memory of political and policy activism as they craft poverty solutions for "the least of these" within their own communities: poor black women and their children. The Poor People's Campaign movement is part of black churches' memory in attempting to secure economic justice, empowering America to make good on its democratic promise to be a land of economic justice for all people. This movement introduced a class-based approach to ending poverty. It introduced a concept of thriving that involved the poor's participation in developing their own capabilities in order to participate on par with their nonpoor peers. Although the PPC was considered unsuccessful and is largely unfinished business today, it can be revived as a vibrant class-based vision of economic justice for our times. We must revive this vision of economic justice if the poor are to become contributing members of our society instead of second-class citizens.

America's democratic project depends in part upon the courageous actions of various communities within civil society and their willingness to say that something is desperately wrong with the way things are in relation to our poor. The strengthening of America's democratic vitalities, then, involves not only the voices of nonreligious communities but also the voices of religious communities. As religious communities, black churches must be willing to strengthen the democratic project in America by decrying how neo-liberal capitalist institutions trick, oppress, and enslave the poor. For example, some black churches are forging a movement that challenges payday-auto-loan shops that exploit the poor (particularly poor blacks) by charging them astronomical interest rates that bury them further in debt. Friendship West Baptist Church in Dallas, Texas, is one black church that has led in confronting the exploitative economic practices of payday loan companies that further intensify deprivation for economically vulnerable people. Friendship West has been at the forefront of protests, marches, and demonstrations against these businesses and is also lobbying for public policy that can regulate these institutions. Confronting these auto-loan sharks and pushing through legislation that places strict regulations on such exploitative companies strengthen democratic rights for the poor in America. The poor are often in such vulnerable economic positions that exploitative business industries such as payday-auto-loan shops are able to take advantage of them with relative ease. This is despicable and unacceptable. The poor can barely survive in an exploitative economic climate that lauds such dehumanizing practices.

Yet, the poor need more than survival. The poor in America need to *thrive*. With threats of cutting Medicaid, education, and other social services by a Republican-controlled Congress, the poor and working class are now faced with increasing material deprivation. They are threatened by the loss of hope in a system that supports the wealthy and rich. Now is the time to *develop a moral consensus* on the problem of poverty and how poverty can be addressed effectively within our nation. Religious institutions can provide leadership in developing a moral consensus on the blight and plight of our poor. Specifically, black churches can begin to rethink their anti-poverty strategies, prosperity theologies, and policy activism in order to participate in a project of hope and thriving with and for poor black women and other poor persons within an American underclass. Resuscitating the PPC would provide black churches with a class-based vision of economic justice that is simultaneously sensitive to how gender and sexuality improve class-based approaches for poor black women. I am afraid that black churches will drift into irrelevancy if they do not become serious about a more healthy gender and sexual politics as they address black women's poverty within this nation.

In addition, I want to note that black churches are part of a number of black socioeconomic and political organizations and institutions that should be in the vanguard in developing a moral consensus on eradicating institutional poverty. As discussed, the black church should no longer be seen as *the* primary site of social and political activism within black communities. The proliferation of other black organizations and institutions such as black banks, black fraternal societies, black political organizations, black think-tanks, and more should collaborate on this class-based vision of economic justice that the PPC introduced. Fashioning forums, round-table discussions, seminars, and consultations on the "means" of this class-based vision of economic justice is needed in order to make thriving a possibility for the poor, such as poor black women. Most important, this movement not only invites the poor to tell their stories of poverty but also invites the poor to be leaders within such movements. The poor's participation in crafting political and policy activism is very important to the integrity, effectiveness, and sustainability of movements oriented toward economic justice. The poor must feel that they have a voice and that they can challenge and transform exploitative socioeconomic attitudes, practices, and institutions.

I am often dismayed that the norms of inclusion and participation among the poor are not taken seriously in present debates surrounding poverty in America. Policymakers and political leaders are quick to diagnose the problem of poverty and offer solutions without ever turning to the lived experiences of the poor. How can such anti-poverty policies be effective if the poor are not consulted on the obstacles they face as well as potential solutions that they are willing to buy into? Because the poor are not treated as subjects, poverty reduction strategies remain ineffective. The poor can be agents of change who take control of their lives if they are given the same ways of access and opportunity that middle- to upper-class persons are given. For instance, I discussed in the previous chapter that the poor's ability to save when offered opportunities to save and invest has been proven. When poor persons in that study were given an opportunity to enhance their lives by access to opportunity, there were high success rates.

The poor must be treated as human beings, not things or objects to be talked about by elite leaders.

I am also deeply aware of the limitations of proffering any asset-building approach to poverty within our present economy, which continues to recover from harsh economic decline. With looming national budget deficits, the request for more money may seem irresponsible and unrealistic. However, what remains irresponsible is asking those who have been hardest hit to sacrifice for the rest of the country (which includes the wealthy). The country must pursue economic recovery and health. However, this cannot come at the expense of the poor. Consequently, the proposal for asset-building approaches to poverty is more of an *invitation to converse about how to give the poor fair access into the wealth-producing structures of our society.* This approach is about attempting to figure out ways to break intergenerational cycles of deprivation. Assets are central. There must be sustained discussions and new proposals on how to include the poor in asset building. This is not only critical for the poor, but it is critical to the future economic and moral health of this nation.

Alongside asset-building policy, promoting socially conscious capitalism is important because it invites discussion on how business communities can participate in poverty amelioration and eradication. When profit maximization is the highest goal of financial companies and businesses, economic attitudes and practices that ignore the poor can be justified. Profit maximization cannot continue to be the primary value within our society. The excessive pursuit of profits must be tempered by values that foster social trust and flourishing for all persons within community. The reduction of poverty cannot happen without economic institutions reconceptualizing how their capitalist efforts can positively affect all people as well as the environment. The possibility of thriving for the poor is not only in the hands of government (at the local, state, and federal levels) but also in the hands of business communities.

It is time to build sustainable movements for economic justice. It is time to join hands and hearts to decry the corruption and greed that continue to threaten the democratic vision that America has yet to fulfill. It is time to reignite the spark for economic justice that the poor require to dislodge themselves and their children from permanent cycles of deprivation. This yearning for economic justice is not experienced just by poor black women; an entire American underclass has been left behind. Black churches can play a significant role in reviving this movement, a movement that can give our children a brighter future and help America to actualize its own commitment to the democratic values of opportunity, liberty, and equality for all. The time is now.

Notes

Introduction

1. Jonathan Walton, *Watch This: The Ethics and Aesthetics of Black Televangelism* (New York: New York University Press, 2009), 231.

2. Karl Marx advocated a particular view of historical materialism. He argued that modes of production determine cultural forms within society (superstructure). The ideological superstructure is no more than a reflection or expression of the material base. Hence, the economic conditions under which society exists are expressed in the superstructure, which radically reduces culture to economic ordering. For Marx, an interpretation of history is singularly based on the material evidence (economics) of how a society is organized. While Frankfurt critical social theorists such as Jürgen Habermas and Walter Benjamin agree with Marx that capitalism and its exploitation of the working and poor classes constitute a large part of the historical capitalist narrative, they challenge Marx in radically reducing culture to economy. For these critical theorists, culture and economy have their own separate orderings but are related and mutually reinforce advanced-capitalist hegemony.

3. Max Pensky, "Method and Time: Benjamin's Dialectical Images," in *The Cambridge Companion to Walter Benjamin*, ed. David Ferris (Cambridge, MA: Cambridge University Press, 2004), 183.

4. Ibid.

5. Ibid.

6. For discussions of advanced capitalism realities, refer also to Jürgen Habermas, *Legitimation Crisis* (Boston: Beacon Press, 1973); idem, *Moral Consciousness and Communicative Action* (Cambridge: The MIT Press, 1990); and idem, *On Pragmatics of Social Interaction* (Cambridge: The MIT Press, 2001)

7. Marx refers to commodity fetishism in his opening chapter of *Das Kapital* (Washington, DC: Regnery Publishing, 2000). Marx describes commodity fetishism as the way in which commodities and money mediate human relationships so that such relationships are emptied of their human value. For example, a $100 note is not really worth $100—it cost only a few cents to produce—but if people accept it as a currency, it can claim $100 worth of goods, in which case it really seems to be worth $100, and the goods seem to be worth $100. Then it seems as if the value of $100 inheres in the money and the goods themselves. The buyer is worth $100 to the seller, and the seller is a $100 expense to the buyer. In considering the trade between buyer and seller, how the buyer and seller are socially related or their identity doesn't really matter, except perhaps for marketing purposes. All that matters is that the $100 note purchases $100 worth of goods.

8. Refer to Dieter Plehwe, Bernhard J. A. Walpen, and Gisela Neunhöffer, eds., *Neoliberal Hegemony: A Global Critique* (New York: Routledge, 2006).

1. Is the Black Church "Home" for Poor Black Women?

1. Barbara Savage, *Your Spirits Walk beside Us: The Politics of Black Religion* (Cambridge, MA: Belknap Press, 2008), 23.

2. Savage, *Your Spirits Walk Beside Us*, 10.

3. The Black Church has been the subject of critical research for over a century. Many black theologians have focused on the subjective aspects of the Black Church. See, for example, Howard Thurman, *Jesus and the Disinherited* (Nashville, TN: Abingdon Press, 1949); James H. Cone, *God of the Oppressed* (Maryknoll, NY: Orbis Books,1975); idem, *For My People: Black Theology and the Black Church: Where Have We Been and Where Are We Going?* (Maryknoll, NY: Orbis Books, 1984); Kelly Brown Douglas, *The Black Christ* (Maryknoll, NY: Orbis Books, 1994). Most recently, there has been interest in the study of the study of the Black Church in *Black Church Studies: An Introduction*, ed. Stacey Floyd-Thomas et al. (Nashville, TN: Abingdon Press, 2007). In addition, black historians and social scientists have focused on the Black Church and its significance for black cultural life in America. Such black scholars include W. E. B. Du Bois in *The Souls of Black Folk* (1903), which was one of the first sociological studies on the Black Church. The most far-reaching study of the Black Church is Carter G. Woodson, *The History of the Negro Church* (Washington, DC: Associated Publishers, 1921). This study is extended in E. Franklin Frazier, *The Negro Church in America* (New York: Schocken Books, 1964); and C. Eric Lincoln and Lawrence Mamiya, *The Black Church in African American Experience* (Durham, NC: Duke University Press, 1990), which is to date the most extensive study of the Black Church.

4. James Gustafson, *Treasure in Earthen Vessels: The Church as a Human Community* (New York: Harper and Row, 1961), ix.

5. Ibid.

6. Ibid.

7. Savage, *Your Spirits Walk beside Us*, 4. For more information on black churches that were emerging in the South for collective political organizing, see William E. Montgomery, *Under Their Own Vine and Fig Tree: The African-American Church in the South, 1865–1900* (Baton Rouge: Louisiana State University Press, 1993); Clarence Walker, *A Rock in a Weary Land: The African Methodist Episcopal Church during the Civil War and Reconstruction* (Baton Rouge: Louisiana State University Press, 1982); and Carol V. R. George, *Segregated Sabbaths: Richard Allen and the Emergence of Independent Black Churches, 1760–1840* (Oxford: Oxford University Press, 1973).

8. Savage, *Your Spirits Walk beside Us*, 6.

9. Ibid.

10. Ibid. For more discussion on the debate that swirled around the political efficacy of black churches, refer to Hans Baer, *The Black Spiritualist Movement: A Religious Response to Racism* (Knoxville: University of Tennessee Press, 1984); Randall Burkett, *Garveyism as a Religious Movement* (Blue Ridge Summit, PA: Scarecrow Press, 1978); C. Eric Lincoln, *The Black Muslims in America* (Grand Rapids, MI: Eerdmans, 1961); and Robert Weisbrot, *Father Divine and the Struggle for Racial Equality* (Champagne: University of Illinois Press, 1983). These texts disclose the judgments of many black groups that the Black Church as an institution failed in responding to the political and economic plight of blacks in America.

11. Savage, *Your Spirits Walk beside Us*, 47. Refer to Carter G. Woodson, *Miseducation of the Negro* (Washington, DC: The Associated Publishers, 1933, 1969), 68.

12. Fannie Williams, quoted in Savage, *Your Spirits Walk beside Us,* 11.

13. Savage, *Your Spirits Walk beside Us,* 13. There were other social scientific studies on black religion that emerged during this time period, including those by Zora Neale Hurston, Arthur Fauset, and Hortense Powerdermaker, all trained ethnographers who studied black religious practices and the relationship among these religious practices, policies, and lived experience. Their work brings one closer to the practices, voices, and ideas of the masses of people within the Black Church.

14. *Eschaton* refers to the end of the present world and is addressed in the study of eschatology, that is, the study of the end times. Within Western Christianity *eschaton* also refers to the day at the end of time following the return of Jesus and the emergence of Armageddon, when God will decree the fates of all individual humans according to the good and evil of their earthly lives. In short, *eschaton* refers to the coming *telos* or end of history in which God will make all things just, peaceful, loving, and right in response to injustice, chaos, hatred, and wrongdoing. For a critical reading of Christian eschatology, refer to Ben Witherington, *Jesus, Paul, and the End of the World* (Downers Grove, IL: InterVarsity Press, 1992).

15. Karen Johnson, *Uplifting the Women and the Race: The Lives, Educational Philosophies, and Social Activism of Anna Julia Cooper and Nannie Helen Burroughs* (New York: Routledge, 2000). The present book discloses my general insight about Nannie Burroughs and her perspective on black churches in relation to transformation.

16. Jonathan Walton, *Watch This!: The Ethics and Aesthetics of Black Televangelism* (New York: New York University, 2009), 177.

17. Ibid., 177-78.

18. Ibid., 178.

19. Peter Paris, *The Social Teaching of the Black Churches* (Philadelphia: Fortress Press, 1985), 10.

20. Ibid., 11.

21. Ibid. Refer to Chapter 5 for further discussion on the Black Church's usage of communal power. A major text that speaks about the black churches' usage of communal power is Albert J. Raboteau, *Slave Religion: The "Invisible Institution" in the Antebellum South* (Oxford: Oxford University Press, 1980).

22. Delores S. Williams, *Sisters in the Wilderness: The Challenge of Womanist God-Talk* (Maryknoll, NY: Orbis Books, 1995), 8-9.

23. Ibid.

24. Cheryl Sanders, *Saints in Exile: The Holiness-Pentecostal Experience in African-American Religion and Culture* (New York: Oxford University Press, 1999), 126.

25. Ibid.

26. Refer to Marcia Riggs, *Awake, Arise, and Act: A Womanist Call for Black Liberation* (Cleveland: Pilgrim Press, 1994). Riggs draws on the black women's club movement in the nineteenth century to provide a means for developing intra-group responsibility that can overcome the discouraging effects of racism, sexism, and classism. While she charts the type of black communal solidarity that black women exhibited across class lines, she bemoans the absence of this solidarity within black communities due to greater class differentiation at the end of the twentieth century.

27. Jacquelyn Grant, "Black Theology and the Black Woman," in *Black Theology: A Documentary History,* ed. Gayraud S. Wilmore and James Cone (Maryknoll, NY: Orbis Books 1993), 325. In *If It Wasn't for the Women* (Maryknoll, NY: Orbis Books, 2000), Cheryl Townsend Gilkes also discusses the contradictions black

women, particularly black women in holiness-Pentecostal traditions, endure within black churches in which they are able to offer their talents and abilities but often under the ecclesial control of black male clergy.

28. Victor Anderson, *Pragmatic Theology: Negotiating the Intersections of an American Philosophy of Religion and Public Theology* (Albany: State University of New York Press, 1998), 59, 114.

29. Victor Anderson, *Creative Exchange: A Constructive Theology of African-American Religious Experience* (Minneapolis: Fortress Press, 2008), 132.

30. Anderson, *Pragmatic Theology*, 59.

31. Ibid.

32. Anderson, *Creative Exchange*, 132.

33. Monica Coleman, an African American female process theologian, expands womanist theological categories in *Making a Way Out of No Way: A Womanist Theology* (Minneapolis: Fortress Press, 2008). She uses process theology as a way to incorporate religious pluralism, sexual diversity, and issues of globalization into the theoretical frameworks of womanist religious discourse. I find Coleman's work compelling on the need for womanist religious discourse to expand its theoretical framework in order to make room for black women's plurality of religious experiences. See also Melanie Harris, *Gifts of Virtue: Alice Walker and Womanist Ethics* (New York: Palgrave Macmillan, 2010), in which Harris argues for the expansion of womanist thought by integrating into its theoretical frameworks the actual inter-religious concerns that Alice Walker possessed when fashioning the term *womanist*. Both Coleman and Harris invite womanist discourse to expand its conceptual categories in order to include religious plurality among black women. In this way womanist discourse is able to include the religious experiences of all black women, not just Christian black women.

34. Marla Frederick, *Between Sundays: Black Women and Everyday Struggles of Faith* (Berkeley and Los Angeles: University of California Press, 2003), 10.

35. Ibid.

36. Ibid., 25.

2. Saving Poor Black Women: Faith-based Initiatives

1. Barbara Ehrenreich, "The Faith Factor," *The Nation* (November 11, 2004), 34. Also see two of Ehrenreich's texts on economic inequality and the government's lack of action in response to such inequalities: *Bait and Switch: The (Futile) Pursuit of the American Dream* (New York: Metropolitan Books, 2006) and *Nickled and Dimed: On (Not) Getting by in America* (New York: Holt Paperbacks, 2008).

2. Ehrenreich, "The Faith Factor," 35.

3. Robert Wuthnow, *Saving America? Faith-Based Services and the Future of Civil Society* (Princeton, NJ: Princeton University Press, 2004), 15.

4. Mimi Abramovitz, *Regulating the Lives of Women: Social Welfare Policy from Colonial Times to the Present* (Cambridge, MA: South End Press, 1988), 75.

5. Ibid., 88.

6. Ibid., 86. For more information on how welfare has been used as a tool of social control by churches and the government, see Frances Fox Piven and Richard A. Cloward, *Regulating the Poor: The Functions of Public Welfare* (New York: Vintage, 1993 reprint). Piven argues that prior to the early sixteenth century, caring for the poor was considered to be primarily the responsibility of the church or of the

rich, who tried to purchase their salvation through almsgiving. Leaving charity to the church meant that few received aid and those not necessarily according to their need. While Piven charts why poverty responses shifted from churches to federal governments, she helpfully describes primary institutions that were responsible for addressing deprivation among the poor in early America: churches.

7. Abramovitz, *Regulating the Lives of Women*, 77.

8. Ibid., 215. For more on conditions that led to a federal welfare state during the Great Depression, refer to William Leuchtenburg, *Franklin D. Roosevelt and the New Deal: 1932-1940* (New York: Harper and Row, 2009).

9. George W. Bush, "Foreword," *Rallying the Armies of Compassion* (Washington, DC, January 2001), 2.

10. Wuthnow, *Saving America?* 65. For more information on how religious communities might be caring communities in relation to faith-based social services, see Mark Chaves, *Congregations in America* (Cambridge, MA: Harvard University Press, 2004); and Ram Canaan et al., *The Invisible Caring Hand: American Congregations and the Provision of Welfare* (New York: New York University Press, 2002).

11. Wuthnow, *Saving America?*, 65.

12. Quoted in ibid., 219.

13. Ibid. For the most comprehensive review and analysis of this survey data about trust refer to Eric Uslaner, *The Moral Foundations of Trust* (Cambridge, UK: Cambridge University Press, 2002). This text gives a more detailed account of both the General Social Survey and Putnam's Social Capital Benchmark survey. The data points to the real significance of religious communities in building cultures of trust that may be useful for social services activities.

14. David Bositis, *Black Churches and the Faith-Based Initiative: Findings from a National Survey* (Washington, DC: The Joint Center for Political and Economic Studies, 2006), 6.

15. Ibid.

16. Ibid.

17. Ibid.

18. Ibid.

19. Ibid.

20. Ibid., 9.

21. Pastor John Marsh, sermon, quoted in Wuthnow, *Saving America?* 67.

22. Ibid.

23. Glenn Loury, quoted in Traci West, *Disruptive Christian Ethics: When Racism and Women's Lives Matter* (Louisville, KY: Westminster John Knox Press, 2006), 95.

24. Ibid.

25. "Remarks by President George Bush at the National Religious Broadcasters' Convention," February 10, 2003, available on the whitehouse.gov website.

26. West, *Disruptive Christian Ethics*, 110.

27. Quoted in West, *Disruptive Christian Ethics*, 110.

28. John Bartkowski and Helen Regis, *Charitable Choices: Religion, Race, and Poverty* (New York: New York University Press, 2003). Moreover, these two authors uncover race factors in how funding in faith-based initiatives is allocated. For instance, they introduce a middle-class African American congregation, River Road UMC, and its black female pastor, Rev. Nancy Evans. Pastor Evans notes that racial problems certainly influence how money is distributed within local religious

communities. She posits that race relations affect the allocation of black grant money to local churches, reifying certain racial and economic inequities among local congregations. Many policymakers of charitable choice are hesitant to allocate needed funds to black churches because black pastors are part time. Their hesitancy is rooted in their tacit assumptions about bi-vocational ministers; they view such ministers as not established or not fully credible. However, within black religious communities, congregations are often unable to support black pastors fully, which means that these religious leaders must secure additional financial means as they provide leadership for their faith community. Consequently, race affects how charitable choice funding is allocated and how programs are implemented. Moreover, such disposition toward black religious leaders also hinders getting help to those communities that may have the most need.

3. We Too Are America

1. Milton Friedman, *Capitalism and Freedom* (Chicago: University of Chicago Press, 1962), 8.

2. Ibid., 13.

3. Ibid.

4. Ibid., 21.

5. Friedman states, "The appropriate recourse of those of us who believe that a particular criterion such as color is irrelevant is to persuade our fellows to be of like mind, not to use the coercive power of the state to force them [capitalists] to act in accordance with our principles" (115).

6. Ibid., 177.

7. Ibid., 178.

8. Refer to these articles on the 2008 Wall Street financial crisis that erupted after a series of deregulation policies: Michael Lewis, "The End" (December 2008), available on the cbsnews.com website; and Sairah Zaidi, "The Wall Street Financial Crisis: What It Means, and Why You Should Care," The Cauldron (September 29, 2008), available on the csucauldron.com website.

9. Dinesh D'Souza, *The End of Racism* (New York: The Free Press, 1995), 477–78.

10. Ibid., 487.

11. Ibid., 481. Prior to the "culture of poverty" explanation in delineating black poverty, a main explanation of black poverty dealt with inferior genes (see Richard Herrnstein and Charles Murray, *The Bell Curve* [New York: Free Press, 1994]). Specifically, they argued that our most exigent social problems, from economic inequality to crime, reflect basic differences in the intellectual abilities of people within a modern society. These intellectual differences are largely due to genetically based differences that can be demonstrated by various types of IQ tests. Hence, for Herrnstein and Murray, racial inequality is a reflection of basic differences that lead to natural inequalities among groups of people. Some scholars argue that the culture-of-poverty argument is a modification of the genes argument, supplanting "the intellectual deficiencies of blacks" with the "cultural deficiencies of blacks." (see Lawrence Harrison, *Who Prospers? How Cultural Values Shape Economic and Political Success* [New York: Basic Books, 1992]).

12. D'Souza, *The End of Racism*, 481.

13. Eugene H. Robinson, *Disintegration: The Splintering of Black America* (New York: Doubleday, 2010), 34.

14. Manning Marable, *How Capitalism Underdeveloped Black America* (Cambridge, MA: South End Press, 1983), 136.

15. Ibid., 162.

16. Ibid., 161–62.

17. Ibid.

18. William Julius Wilson, *The Declining Significance of Race: Blacks and Changing American Institutions* (Chicago: University of Chicago Press, 1980), 152.

19. Ibid.

20. Teresa Amott, "Black Women and AFDC," in *Women, the State, and Welfare*, ed. Linda Gordon (Milwaukee: University of Wisconsin Press, 1990), 286.

21. Ibid., 287.

22. Amott's central point is that a structural analysis of poor black women within urban areas must not only take account of oppressive structures and systems that impede these women's well-being but also consider the agential capacities of poor black women despite such structural oppressions. This argument should be distinguished from other arguments, such as that of Robert Woodson (founder of National Center for Neighborhood Enterprise), who contends that more responsibility should be placed on the agential capacities of these poor women. Clearly, Woodson's argument contrasts with Amott's point, namely, that *within a structural analysis of poverty among black women, an account of their agency is required.*

23. William Julius Wilson, *The Truly Disadvantaged: The Inner City, the Underclass, and Public Policy* (Chicago: University of Chicago Press, 1987), 8.

24. Ibid. See also Douglas G. Glasgow's *Black Underclass* (New York: Vintage Books, 1981). Glasgow separates the black "underclass" from lower-income blacks by several rough social criteria: an absence of generational socioeconomic upward mobility, the lack of real opportunities to succeed, and widespread anger and despair, which arises from contact with mainstream institutions that economically, politically, and socially (albeit impersonally) reject them.

25. See "Class Struggle and Modes of Production," "Capital, Volume One" and "Capital, Volume Three," in *The Marx-Engels Reader*, 2nd ed., ed. Robert C. Tucker (New York: W. W. Norton and Company, 1978).

26. These four basic conditions are derived from Wilson's description of the underclass in *The Truly Disadvantaged*. He states that the underclass refers to inner-city neighborhoods "that are populated almost exclusively by the most disadvantaged segments of the black community, that heterogeneous grouping of families and individuals who are outside the mainstream occupational system. Included in this group are individuals who lack training and skills and either experience long-term unemployment or are not members of the labor force, individuals who are engaged in street crime and other forms of aberrant behavior, and families that experience long-term spells of poverty and/or welfare dependency. . . . I use this term to depict a reality not captured in the more standard designation *lower class*" (7–8).

27. Marcellus Andrews, *The Political Economy of Hope and Fear: Capitalism and the Black Condition in America* (New York: New York University, 2001), 3.

28. Ibid.

29. Wilson, *The Truly Disadvantaged*, 102.

30. Ibid.

31. Ibid., 103. Also see Jonathan Kozol, *Savage Inequalities* (New York: Crown Publishers, 1991). Kozol discloses the racism in urban education that continues to disadvantage black youth.

32. William Julius Wilson, *When Work Disappears: The World of the New Urban Poor* (New York: Knopf Random House, 1996), 30.

33. Ibid., 32.

34. Marla F. Frederick, *Between Sundays: Black Women and Everyday Struggles of Faith* (Berkeley and Los Angeles: University of California Press, 2003).

35. Wilson, *When Work Disappears*, 30.

36. Marable, *How Capitalism Underdeveloped Black America*, 58.

37. US Census Bureau, *Income, Expenditures, Poverty, and Wealth: Poverty, 2009* (December 2010), Current Population Reports, 464, and Historical Tables, Table 711, available on the census.gov website.

38. Patricia Hill Collins, "Gender, Black Feminism, and Black Political Economy," *Annals of the American Academy of Political and Social Science* 568 (March 2000): 47.

39. Julianne Malveaux, *Slipping through the Cracks: The Status of Black Women* (New Brunswick, NJ: Transaction Books, 1986), 26.

40. Monica Jackson, "And Still We Rise: African American Women and the US Labor Market," in *Gender Issues* 10/2 (Fall 1990): 59.

41. Laura Fitzpatrick, "Why Do Women Still Earn Less Than Men?" *Time Magazine* (April 2011).

42. For greater historical analysis on the percentage of black homes headed by single women and the effect on black families, see A. L. Ferris, *Indicators of Trends in the Status of American Women* (New York: Russell Sage, 1973).

43. Jesse Washington, "Blacks Struggle with 72 Percent Unwed Mothers Rate," *Associated Press* (November 7, 2010).

44. Collins, "Gender, Black Feminism, and Black Political Economy," 45.

45. Ibid.

46. Welfare here is articulated as public assistance for poor, single women although welfare refers to an array of programs that aid women, children, the elderly, disabled people, and more. For a historical view of welfare policy in America and its relationship to race, class, and gender, see Mimi Abramovitz, *Regulating the Lives of Women: Social Welfare Policy from Colonial Times to the Present* (Boston: South End Press, 1988); idem, *Under Attack, Fighting Back: Women and Welfare in the United States* (New York: Monthly Review Press, 1996); and idem, *The Dynamics of Social Welfare Policy* (Oxford: Oxford University Press, 2007). These texts also address white women, the population that welfare policy has historically aided the most. For a discussion on how political economy has adversely affected black women, contributing to their welfare enrollments, see David Hilfiker, *Urban Injustice: How Ghettos Happen* (New York: Seven Stories Press, 2003), chap. 4.

47. United States Department of Labor, "The Black Labor Force in Recovery Report," Office of Secretary webpage, available on the dol.gov website.

48. Marian Wright Edelman, *Families in Peril: An Agenda for Social Change* (Cambridge, MA: Harvard University Press, 1987), 3.

49. Ibid., 4.

50. Ibid., 5.

51. Marian Wright Edelman, "The Black Community Crusade for Children," *Huffington Post Internet Newspaper*, posted January 19, 2011.

52. Annette Lareau, *Unequal Childhoods: Class, Race, and Family Life* (Berkeley and Los Angeles: University of California Press, 2003), 15.

53. Ibid., 18.

54. Ibid.

55. Ibid.

56. Ibid.

57. Ibid., 22.

58. Carl Husemoller Nightingale, *On the Edge: A History of Poor Black Children and Their American Dreams* (New York: Basic Books, 1993), 48.

59. Ibid.

60. Andrews, *The Political Economy of Hope and Fear*, 167.

4. Guilty until Proven Innocent

1. Emilie Townes, *Womanist Ethics and the Cultural Production of Evil* (New York: Palgrave Macmillan, 2006), 129.

2. Marvin Olasky, *The Tragedy of American Compassion* (Wheaton, IL: Crossway Books, 2008), 23.

3. Mark Beliles and Stephen McDowell, *America's Providential History* (Charlottesville: The Providence Foundation, 1991).

4. Ibid., 214–15.

5. Ibid., 197.

6. In Anthony Pinn, "Warm Bodies, Cold Currency: A Study of Religion's Response to Poverty," in *Religion and Poverty: Pan-African Perspectives*, ed. Peter Paris (Durham, NC: Duke University Press Books, 2009), 106–7.

7. Ibid., 124.

8. Traci West, "Agenda for Churches: Uprooting a National Policy of Morally Stigmatizing Poor Single Black Moms," in *Welfare Policy: Feminist Critiques,* ed. Elizabeth Bounds, Pamela Brubaker, and Mary Hobgood (Cleveland: Pilgrim Press, 1999), 133.

9. Ibid., 136.

10. Ibid., 137.

11. Townes, *Womanist Ethics and the Cultural Production of Evil*, 115.

12. Ibid.

13. Mimi Abramovitz, *Under Attack, Fighting Back: Women and Welfare in the United States* (New York: Monthly Review Press, 1996), 215.

14. Ibid.

15. Ibid.

16. Ibid.

17. Ibid.

18. Ibid.

19. Michael Katz, *The Undeserving Poor: From the War on Poverty to the War on Welfare* (New York: Pantheon Books, 1990), 54. Katz also provides a rich discussion of how colonial relief among the poor created moral distinctions between the materially advantaged and the poor, in which the poor were seen as morally inferior. See Michael Katz, *In the Shadow of the Poorhouse: A Social History of Welfare in America* (New York: Basic Books, 1996); and idem, *The Price of Citizenship: Redefining the American Welfare State* (New York: Henry Holt and Company, 2008).

20. Katz, *The Undeserving Poor,* 54.

21. Walter Trattner, *From Poor Law to Welfare State: A History of Welfare in America,* 6th ed. (New York: The Free Press, 1998), 364.

22. Ibid.

23. Ibid. Also see Ralph Dolgoff and Donald Feldstein, *Understanding Social Welfare: A Search for Social Justice* (London: Allyn and Bacon, 2008).

24. Donald Barlett and James Steele, *The Great American Tax Dodge: How Spiraling Fraud and Avoidance Are Killing Fairness, Destroying the Income Tax, and Costing You* (Berkeley and Los Angeles: University of California Press, 2002). There were also a number of articles in *USA Today* in 2011 that revealed tax fraud and evasion among wealthy members within society. For one example of how tax fraud and evasion are far more costly to American taxpayers than public welfare assistance, see "US Officials Charge 4 Swiss Bankers in Tax Evasion," *USA Today* (February 23, 2011).

25. Michelle Alexander, *The New Jim Crow: Mass Incarceration in the Age of Colorblindness* (New York: The New Press, 2010), 33.

26. Julia Sudbury, *Global Lockdown: Race, Gender, and the Prison Industrial Complex* (New York: Routledge, 2005), 26. Sudbury writes that rising rates of incarceration among these women is not an American phenomenon, but a global phenomenon deeply tied to poverty and inequality.

27. Ibid.

28. Ibid., 54.

29. Ibid.

30. Ibid.

31. Ibid.

32. Beth Richie, *Compelled to Crime: The Gender Entrapment of Battered Black Women* (New York: Routledge, 1996), 56. Also refer to Marjorie Valbrun, "States: Food Stamp, Welfare Bans for Drug Felons Counterproductive," in *America's Wire* (April 9, 2011).

33. For more discussion of this topic, see Iris Lopez, "Sterilization among Puerto Rican Women in New York City: Public Policy and Social Constraints," in *Cities of the United States: Studies in Urban Anthropology,* ed. Leith Mullings (New York: Columbia University Press, 1987); and Jessie Rodrique, "The Black Community and the Birth-Control Movement," in *Unequal Sisters: A Multi-Cultural Reader in U.S. Women's History,* ed. Ellen Carol Dubois and Vicki L. Ruiz (New York: Routledge, 1990).

34. Dorothy Roberts, *Killing the Black Body: Race, Reproduction, and the Meaning of Liberty* (New York: Vintage Books, 1997), 210.

35. Dána-Ain Davis, *Battered Black Women and Welfare Reform: Between a Rock and a Hard Place* (Albany: State University of New York Press, 2006), 45.

36. Wahneema Lubiano, "Black Ladies, Welfare Queens, and State Minstrels: Ideological Wars by Narrative Means," in *Race-ing Justice, En-gendering Power: Essays on Anita Hill, Clarence Thomas and the Construction of Social Reality,* ed. Toni Morrison (New York: Pantheon Books, 1992), 339.

37. Davis, *Battered Black Women and Welfare Reform,* 43.

38. George Gilder, *Wealth and Poverty* (New York: Basic Books, 1981), 136.

39. Lawrence Mead, *Beyond Entitlement: The Social Obligations of Citizenship* (New York: Free Press, 1986), 126.

40. Ibid.

41. Davis, *Battered Black Women and Welfare Reform,* 68.

42. Davis's ethnographic study attempts to protect the women she interviewed, who are victims of domestic violence. The names of the women she interviewed have been changed, and in addition, Lanville, New York, is a fictional city name for the city where she did her field work with these women.

43. Davis, *Battered Black Women and Welfare Reform*, 70.

44. Ibid.

45. Ibid., 107–8.

46. Quoted in Davis, *Battered Black Women and Welfare Reform*, 108. This quotation was part of the ethnographic study that Davis foregrounds in this text.

47. Ibid., 108, 125.

48. For these statistics, refer to Callie Marie Rennison and Sarah Welchans, "Intimate Partner Violence," US Department of Justice, *Bureau of Justice Statistics*, NCJ-178247 (May 2000).

49. Davis, *Battered Black Women and Welfare Reform*, 13.

50. Ibid.

51. Ibid., 86.

52. Martha Davis and Susan Kraham, "Protecting Women's Welfare in the Face of Violence," *Fordham Urban Law Journal* 22/4 (1995): 33.

53. Ibid., 26.

54. Ibid.

55. Demie Kurz, "Women, Welfare, and Domestic Violence," in *Whose Welfare?* ed. Gwendolyn Mink (Ithaca, NY: Cornell University Press, 1999), 145.

56. Joy James, *Resisting State Violence: Radicalism, Gender, and Race in US Culture* (Minneapolis: University of Minnesota Press, 1996), 73.

57. Linda Ammons, "Mules, Madonnas, Babies, Bathwater, Racial Imagery, and Stereotypes: The African-American Woman and the Battered Woman Syndrome," *Wisconsin Law Review* (1995): 58.

58. Evelyn Barbee, "Ethnicity and Woman Abuse in the United States," in *Violence against Women: Nursing Research, Education, and Practice Issues*, ed. Carolyn Sampselle (New York: Hemisphere Publishing Corporation), 155, 158.

5. The Unfinished Business of the Poor People's Campaign

1. Gerald McKnight, *The Last Crusade: Martin Luther King, Jr., the FBI, and the Poor People's Campaign* (Boulder, CO: Westview Press, 1998), 14–15. Also refer to Adam Fairclough, *To Redeem the Soul of America: The Southern Christian Leadership Conference and Martin Luther King, Jr.* (Athens: University of Georgia Press, 1978); and Martin Luther King, Jr., *Why We Can't Wait* (New York: Signet Classics, 1964). These texts explore, in part, tensions that existed within black communities concerning SCLC's methods of nonviolent direct protests, marches, and boycotts.

2. McKnight, *The Last Crusade*, 15.

3. Ibid., 14–15. Also see Carl T. Rowan, *Breaking Barriers: A Memoir* (New York: Little Brown and Company, 1991); and James Melvin Washington, ed., *A Testament of Hope: The Essential Writings of Martin Luther King, Jr.* (New York: HarperCollins, 1991). These texts also explore how some conservative black communities and churches saw their social role, which was primarily non-radical and non-confrontational to the larger social system.

4. McKnight, *The Last Crusade*, 15.

5. Septima Clark, *Ready from Within: Septima Clark and the Civil Rights Movement, A First Person Narrative*, ed. Cynthia Stokes Brown (Trenton, NJ: Africa World Press, 1990), 15. For more on Clark's critique of SCLC organizational model and methods of protest, see Katherine Mellen Charon, *Freedom's Teacher: The Life of Septima Clark* (Charlotte: University of North Carolina Press, 2009).

6. Rosetta Ross, *Witnessing and Testifying: Black Women, Religion, and Civil Rights* (Minneapolis: Fortress Press, 2003), 43.

7. Ibid. For more on the importance of educational citizenship programs for blacks in regard to the ballot, see Clayborne Carson, *In Struggle: SNCC and the Black Awakening of the 1960s* (Cambridge, MA: Harvard University Press, 1981).

8. Ross, *Witnessing and Testifying*, 45.

9. Ibid.

10. Ibid.

11. Joanne Grant, *Ella Baker: Freedom Bound* (New York: John Wiley and Sons, 1998), 83. Also refer to these following texts for more on Ella Baker's leadership and ideas of participatory democracy within SNCC: Howard Zinn, *The New Abolitionists* (Cambridge: South End Press, 1965); Cheryl Lynn, ed., *A Circle of Trust: Remembering SNCC* (Piscataway, NJ: Rutgers University Press, 1998); Mary King, *Freedom Song: A Personal History of the 1960s Civil Rights Movement* (New York: William Morrow and Company, 1987); and John Lewis, *Walking with the Wind: A Memoir of the Movement* (New York: Simon and Schuster, 1998).

12. Grant, *Ella Baker*, 83.

13. Ibid.

14. Johnnetta Betsch Cole and Beverly Guy-Sheftall, *Gender Talk: The Struggle for Women's Equality in African American Communities* (New York: Ballantine Books, 2003), 73.

15. Paula Giddings, *When and Where I Enter: The Impact of Black Women on Race and Sex in America* (New York: William Morrow Publishers, 1984).

16. Cole and Guy-Sheftall, *Gender Talk*, 84.

17. In ibid.

18. Ibid.

19. Ibid.

20. Ibid.

21. Ibid.

22. Ibid.

23. Ibid., 127. For information on the gender politics within the Civil Rights and Black Power movements, refer to Toni Cade, ed., *The Black Woman: An Anthology* (New York: Washington Square Press, 1970); Michele Wallace, *Black Macho and the Myth of the Superwoman* (New York: Warner Books, 1979); Sarah Evans, *Personal Politics: The Roots of Women's Liberation in the Civil Rights Movement and the New Left* (New York: Vintage Books, 1979); Donna Franklin, *What's Love Got to Do with It* (New York: Simon and Schuster, 2000); Deborah Gray White, *Too Heavy a Load: Black Women in Defense of Themselves, 1894–1994* (New York: W. W. Norton & Company, 1999); and Belinda Robnett, *How Long? How Long?: African American Women in the Struggle for Civil Rights* (Oxford: Oxford University Press, 1997).

24. Height, in Cole and Guy-Sheftall, *Gender Talk*, 86.

25. Cole and Guy-Sheftall, *Gender Talk*, 86.

26. Ibid.

27. Ibid.

28. Ibid.

29. John D'Emilio, *Lost Prophet: The Life and Times of Bayard Rustin* (New York: Free Press, 2003), 165.

30. Jervis Anderson, *Bayard Rustin: Troubles I've Seen* (Berkeley and Los Angeles: University of California Press, 1998), 234.

31. Cole and Sheftall, *Gender Talk*, 155.

32. Johnnetta Cole, quoted in ibid.

33. Some of these critical texts include Stephen O. Murray and Will Roscoe, eds., *Boy-Wives and Female Husbands: Studies of African Homosexualities* (New York: Palgrave, 1998); Evelyn Blackwood, ed., *The Many Faces of Homosexuality* (New York: Routledge, 1986); Wayne Dynes and S. Donaldson, *Ethnographic Studies of Homosexuality* (Oxford: Garland Science, 1992); and Mark Gevisser and Edwin Cameron, eds., *Defiant Desire: Gay and Lesbian Lives in South Africa* (New York: Routledge, 1995).

34. Gloria Wekker, "*Mati*-ism and Black Lesbianism: Two Idealtypical Expressions of Female Homosexuality in Black Communities of the Diaspora," in *The Greatest Taboo: Homosexuality in Black Communities*, ed. Delroy Constantine Simms (Los Angeles: Alyson Books, 2001), 149.

35. Patricia Hill Collins, *Black Sexual Politics: African Americans, Gender, and the New Racism* (New York: Routledge, 2004), 186.

36. Ibid.

37. Ibid., 205.

38. See McKnight, *The Last Crusade*, 4.

39. Martin Luther King, Jr., "Why I Am Opposed to the War in Vietnam," sermon delivered on April 30, 1967, at Riverside Church, New York.

40. McKnight, *The Last Crusade*, 4.

41. Ibid., 18.

42. Ibid.

43. Ibid., 20.

44. Ibid.

45. Ibid.

46. Ibid., 22.

47. Ibid.

48. Ibid., 2.

49. Ibid.

50. Ibid.

51. Ralph Abernathy, quoted in ibid., 9.

52. Ralph Abernathy, *And the Walls Came Tumbling Down: An Autobiography* (New York: HarperCollins, 1991), 502.

53. McKnight, *The Last Crusade*, 113.

54. Ibid.

55. Ibid., 114.

56. Ibid.

57. Ibid.

58. Ibid.

59. Ibid., 130.

60. Ibid.

61. Ibid., 129.

62. See Kelly Brown Douglas, *Sexuality and the Black Church: A Womanist Perspective* (Maryknoll, NY: Orbis Books, 1999); and idem, *What's Faith Got to Do with It? Black Bodies/Christian Souls* (Maryknoll, NY: Orbis Books, 2005).

6. A New Kind of Prosperity Gospel

1. Shayne Lee, *America's New Preacher: T. D. Jakes* (New York: New York University Press, 2005), 9.

2. Ibid., 100.

3. Ibid.

4. Ibid.

5. Ibid.

6. Ibid.

7. Ibid., 115.

8. Ibid.

9. Ibid.

10. Irving Wohlfarth, "The Measure of the Possible, the Weight of the Real, and the Heat of the Moment: Benjamin's Actuality Today," in *The Actuality of Walter Benjamin*, ed. Laura Marcus and Lynda Nead (London: Lawrence and Wishart, 1998), 27.

11. Walter Benjamin, "Theses on the Philosophy of History," in *Illuminations: Essays and Reflections*, ed. Hannah Arendt (New York: Harcourt Brace Jovanovich, 1968), 258.

12. Ibid.

13. Wohlfarth, "The Measure of the Possible, the Weight of the Real, and the Heat of the Moment," 27.

14. Jürgen Habermas, "Walter Benjamin: Consciousness-Raising or Rescuing Critique," in *On Walter Benjamin: Critical Essays and Recollections*, ed. Gary Smith (Cambridge, MA: MIT Press, 1991), 136–37. For more information on the function of dream images in Benjamin's work, see Susan Buck-Morss, *The Dialectics of Seeing: Walter Benjamin and the Arcades Projects* (Cambridge, MA: The MIT Press, 1989).

15. Wohlfarth, "The Measure of the Possible, the Weight of the Real, and the Heat of the Moment," 27.

16. Zygmunt Bauman, "Walter Benjamin, the Intellectual," in *The Actuality of Walter Benjamin*, ed. Laura Marcus and Lynda Nead (London: Lawrence and Mishart, 1998), 75.

17. Ibid.

18. Max Pensky, "Method and Time: Benjamin's Dialectical Images," in *The Cambridge Introduction to Walter Benjamin*, ed. David Ferris (Cambridge: Cambridge University Press, 2008), 192.

19. Ibid.

20. Bauman, "Walter Benjamin, the Intellectual," 76.

21. Ibid., 77.

22. David Ferris, *The Cambridge Introduction to Walter Benjamin* (Cambridge: Cambridge University Press, 2008), 78.

23. Iva Jevtic, "Between Word and Image: Walter Benjamin's Images as Species of Space," 5, available on the inter-disciplinary.net website.

24. Monica Coleman, *Making a Way Out of No Way: A Womanist Theology* (Minneapolis: Fortress Press, 2008), 103.

25. See Emilie Townes, *Womanist Justice, Womanist Hope* (Atlanta: Scholars Press, 1993); idem, *Embracing the Spirit: Womanist Perspectives on Hope, Salvation, and Transformation* (Maryknoll, NY: Orbis Books, 1997); Karen Baker-Fletcher, *Sisters of Dust, Sisters of Spirit: Womanist Words on God and Creation* (Minneapolis: Fortress Press, 1998); and Katie Cannon, *Katie's Canon: Womanism and*

the Soul of the Black Community (Minneapolis: Fortress Press, 1998). These texts provide illuminating arguments on the significance of past black women's histories and narratives, such as Ida B. Wells and Zora Neale Hurston. The memories and legacies of these past women make a claim upon the prospects of hope and justice for black women and contemporary black communities. See also Marcia Y. Riggs, ed., *Can I Get a Witness: Prophetic Religious Voices of African American Women, an Anthology,* (Maryknoll, NY: Orbis Books, 1997).

26. bell hooks, *Salvation: Black People and Love* (New York: Perennial, 2001), 3–4.

27. Dale Andrews, *Practical Theology for Black Churches: Bridging Black Theology and African-American Folk Religion* (Louisville, KY: Westminster John Knox Press, 2002), 65.

7. An Asset-Building Policy Approach

1. Nancy Fraser and Axel Honneth, *Redistribution or Recognition: A Political-Philosophical Exchange* (New York: Verso, 2003), 9.

2. Ibid., 36.

3. Ibid.

4. Ibid.

5. Ibid., 43.

6. Seyla Benhabib, *Situating the Self: Gender, Community, and Postmodernism in Contemporary Ethics* (New York: Routledge, 1992), 127.

7. Martha Nussbaum argues that the poor can thrive only through developing their central human capabilities. She identifies a list of central capabilities that the global poor (particular poor women) need to flourish, including bodily health, bodily integrity, senses/imagination/thought, emotions, practical reason, affiliation, other species, play, and control over one's environment (*Women and Human Development: The Capabilities Approach* [Cambridge: Cambridge University Press, 2000]; for an in-depth description of each human capability, see chap. 1).

8. Fraser and Honneth, *Redistribution or Recognition,* 3.

9. Ibid.

10. Ibid., 4.

11. Ibid.

12. James Bailey, *Rethinking Poverty: Income, Assets, and the Catholic Social Justice Tradition* (Notre Dame, IN: University of Notre Dame Press, 2010), 9.

13. Ibid., 12.

14. Ibid.

15. Ibid., 13.

16. Edward Scanlon and Deborah Page-Adams, "Effects of Asset Holding on Neighborhoods, Families, and Children: A Review of the Research," in *Building Assets: A Report on the Asset-Development and IDA Field,* ed. Ray Boshara (Washington, DC: Corporation for Enterprise Development, 2001), 38.

17. Michael Sherraden, *Assets and the Poor: A New American Welfare Policy* (Armonk, NY: M. E. Sharpe, 1991), 147–67.

18. The Pew Research Center, "Wealth Gap Rises to Record Highs between Whites, Blacks, and Hispanics (July 26, 2011). This report emphasizes how non-economic variables such as discrimination hinder asset building for these minorities. See also Melvin Oliver and Thomas Shapiro, *Black Wealth/White Wealth: A New Perspective on Racial Inequality* (New York: Routledge, 1995).

19. Trina Williams Shanks, "The Homestead Act: A Major Asset-Building Policy in American History," in *Inclusion in the American Dream: Assets, Poverty, and Public Policy*, ed. Michael Sherraden (New York: Oxford University, 2005), 29.

20. Ibid.

21. Ibid.

22. Ibid.

23. Ibid., 32.

24. Ibid.

25. Ibid.

26. Claude F. Ourbre, *Forty Acres and a Mule: The Freedmen's Bureau and Black Land Ownership* (Baton Rouge: Louisiana State University Press, 1978), 31.

27. Ibid.

28. Ibid., 159.

29. W. E. B. Du Bois, *The Souls of Black Folk* (Chicago: A. C. McClurg and Co., 1903), 33.

30. Oliver and Shapiro, *Black Wealth/White Wealth*, 38.

31. Douglas Massey and Nancy Denton, *American Apartheid: Segregation and the Making of the Underclass* (Cambridge, MA: Harvard University Press, 1993), 36.

32. Ibid.

33. Ibid.

34. Sairah Zaidi, "The Wall Street Financial Crisis: What It Means, and Why You Should Care," *The Cauldron* (September 29, 2008), available on the media. www.csucauldron.com website.

35. Dalton Conley, *Being Black, Living in the Red: Race, Wealth, and Social Policy in America* (Berkeley and Los Angeles: University of California Press, 1999), 25.

36. Ibid.

37. Ray Boshara, "Combating Poverty by Building Assets: Lessons from around the World," *Pathways* (Spring 2009): 22.

38. Ibid.

39. Ibid.

40. Ibid., 24.

41. Mark Schreiner and Michael Sherraden, *Can the Poor Save? Saving and Asset Building in Individual Development Accounts* (London: Transaction, 2007), 1.

42. Ibid., 26.

43. Robert Lerman and Signe-Mary McKernan, "Benefits and Consequences of Holding Assets," in *Asset Building and Low Income Families*, ed. Signe-Mary McKernan and Michael Sherraden (Washington, DC: Urban Institute Press, 2008), 198.

44. Ibid.

45. Muhammad Yunus, *Building Social Business: The New Kind of Capitalism that Serves Humanity's Most Pressing Needs* (New York: Public Affairs, 2010), 14.

46. See Muhammad Yunus, *Creating a World without Poverty: Social Business and the Future of Capitalism* (New York: Public Affairs, 2007), 33.

47. Yunus, *Building Social Business*, 54.

48. Ibid.

Epilogue: Building a Movement to End Poverty

1. "Census Data: Half of U.S. Poor or Low Income," *CBSNews* (December 15, 2011). Available online.

Suggested Readings

On the Black Church

Andrews, Dale. *Practical Theology for Black Churches: Bridging Black Theology and African-American Folk Religion*. Louisville, KY: Westminster John Knox Press, 2002.

Drake, St. Clair, and Horace R. Cayton. *Black Metropolis: A Study of Negro Life in a Northern City*. Reprint Chicago: University of Chicago Press, 1993; originally published 1945.

Frederick, Marla. *Between Sundays: Black Women and Everyday Struggles of Faith*. Berkeley and Los Angeles: University of California Press, 2003.

Lee, Shayne. *America's New Preacher: T. D. Jakes*. New York: New York University Press, 2005.

Myrdal, Gunnar. *An American Dilemma: The Negro Problem and Modern Democracy*. Original study 1944.

Paris, Peter. *The Social Teachings of the Black Church*. Philadelphia: Fortress Press, 1985.

Savage, Barbara. *Your Spirits Walk beside Us: The Politics of Black Religion*. Cambridge, MA: Belknap Press, 2008.

Thomas, Linda. *Living Stones in the Household of God: The Legacy and Future of Black Theology*. Minneapolis: Fortress Press, 2004.

West, Traci. "Agenda for the Churches: Uprooting a National Policy of Morally Stigmatizing Poor Single Black Moms." In *Welfare Policy: Feminist Critiques*, edited by Elizabeth Bounds, Pamela Brubaker, and Mary Hobgood, 220-38. Cleveland: Pilgrim Press, 1999.

On Race

Alexander, Michelle. *The New Jim Crow: Mass Incarceration in the Age of Colorblindness*. New York: The New Press, 2010.

Anderson, Victor. *Beyond Ontological Blackness: An Essay on African American Religious Criticism*. New York: Continuum, 1998.

————. *Creative Exchange: A Constructive Theology of African American Religious Experience*. Minneapolis: Fortress Press, 2008.

Collins, Patricia Hill. *Black Sexual Politics: African Americans, Gender, and the New Racism*. New York: Routledge, 2004.

Baker-Fletcher, Karen. "The Difference Race Makes." *Journal of Feminist Studies in Religion* 8, no. 2 (1992): 7-15.

On Gender and Sexuality

Cole, Johnnetta Betsch, and Beverly Guy-Sheftall. *Gender Talk: The Struggle for Women's Equality in African American Communities*. New York: Ballantine Books, 2003.

D'Emilio, John. *Lost Prophet: The Life and Times of Bayard Rustin*. New York: The Free Press, 2003.

Douglas, Kelly Brown. *Sexuality and the Black Church: A Womanist Perspective*. Maryknoll, NY: Orbis Books, 1999.

Lubiano, Wahneema. "Black Ladies, Welfare Queens, and State Minstrels: Ideological Wars by Narrative Means." In *Race-ing Justice, En-gendering Power: Essays on Anita Hill, Clarence Thomas and the Construction of Social Reality*, edited by Toni Morrison. New York: Pantheon Books, 1992.

Thomas, Linda. "Womanist Theology, Epistemology, and a New Anthropological Paradigm." *CrossCurrents* 48, no. 4 (Winter 1998-1999): 7-13.

Wekker, Gloria. "*Mati*-ism and Black Lesbianism: Two Idealtypical Expressions of Female Homosexuality in Black Communities of the Diaspora." In *The Greatest Taboo: Homosexuality in Black Communities*, edited by Delroy Constantine Simms, 125-59. Los Angeles: Alyson Books, 2001.

On Poverty

Katz, Michael. *Improving Poor People*. Princeton, NJ: Princeton University Press, 1995.

Malveaux, Julianne, and Margaret C. Simms. *Slipping through the Cracks: The Status of Black Women*. New Brunswick, NJ: Transaction Books, 1986.

Nightingale, Carl Husemoller. *On the Edge: A History of Poor Black Children and Their American Dreams*. New York: Basic Books, 1993.

Piven, Frances Fox, and Richard Cloward. *Regulating the Poor: The Functions of Public Welfare*. New York: Pantheon Books, 1971.

Wilson, William Julius. *The Truly Disadvantaged: The Inner City, the Underclass, and Public Policy*. Chicago: University of Chicago Press, 1987.

On the Poor People's Campaign

Abernathy, Ralph. *And the Walls Came Tumbling Down: An Autobiography*. New York: HarperCollins, 1991.

McKnight, Gerald. *The Last Crusade: Martin Luther King, Jr., the FBI, and the Poor People's Campaign*. Boulder, CO: Westview Press, 1998.

Ross, Rosetta E. *Witnessing and Testifying: Black Women, Religion, and Civil Rights*. Minneapolis: Fortress Press, 2006.

On Welfare Policy

Abramovitz, Mimi. *Regulating the Lives of Women: Social Welfare Policy from Colonial Times to Present*. New York: South End Press, 1996.

Davis, Dána-Ain. *Battered Black Women and Welfare Reform: Between a Rock and a Hard Place*. Albany: State University of New York Press, 2006.

Kurz, Demie. "Women, Welfare, and Domestic Violence." In *Whose Welfare?*, edited by Gwendolyn Mink. Ithaca, NY: Cornell University Press, 1999.
Neubeck, Kenneth. *Welfare Racism: Playing the Race Card against America's Poor.* New York: Routledge, 2001.
Quadagno, Jill. *The Color of Welfare: How Racism Undermined the War on Poverty.* Oxford: Oxford University Press, 1994.

On the Economy

Friedman, Milton. *Capitalism and Freedom.* Chicago: University of Chicago Press, 1962.
Wallace, Phyllis. *Black Women in the Labor Force.* Boston: MIT Press, 1980.
Wilson, William Julius. *The Declining Significance of Race: Blacks and Changing American Institutions.* Chicago: University of Chicago, 1978.
———. *When Work Disappears: The World of the New Urban Poor.* New York: Knopf, 1996.

On Critical Social Theory

Arato, Andrew, and Eike Gebhardt, eds. *The Essential Frankfurt School Reader.* New York: Continuum Publishing Company, 2005.
Ferris, David. *The Cambridge Introduction to Walter Benjamin.* Cambridge: Cambridge University Press, 2008.
Fraser, Nancy, and Axel Honneth. *Redistribution or Recognition: A Political-Philosophical Exchange.* New York: Verso, 2003.
Marcus, Laura, and Lynda Nead, eds. *The Actuality of Walter Benjamin.* London: Lawrence and Wishart, 1998.

On Democratic Practices

Benhabib. Seyla, ed. *Democracy and Difference: Contesting the Boundaries of the Political.* Princeton, NJ: Princeton University Press, 1996.
Fraser, Nancy. *Unruly Practices: Power, Discourse, and Gender in Contemporary Social Theory.* Cambridge, UK: Polity Press, 1989.
West, Cornel. *Democracy Matters: Winning the Fight against Imperialism.* New York: Penguin, 2004.
Young, Iris. *Justice and the Politics of Difference.* Princeton, NJ: Princeton University Press, 1990.

On Asset-Building Approaches

Bailey, James. *Rethinking Poverty: Income, Assets, and the Catholic Social Justice Tradition.* Notre Dame, IN: University of Notre Dame Press, 2010.
Ourbre, Claude. *Forty Acres and a Mule: The Freedmen's Bureau and Black Land Ownership.* Baton Rouge: Louisiana State University Press, 1978.
Schreiner, Mark, and Michael Sherraden. *Can the Poor Save? Saving and Asset Building in Individual Development Accounts.* London: Transaction, 2007.

Sherraden, Michael. *Assets and the Poor: A New American Welfare Policy.* Armonk, NY: M. E. Sharpe, 1991.

On Black Feminist and Womanist Ethics

hooks, bell. *Rock My Soul: Black People and Self-Esteem.* New York: Atria Books, 2003.
Riggs, Marcia. *Awake, Arise, and Act: A Womanist Call for Black Liberation.* Cleveland: Pilgrim Press, 1994.
Townes, Emilie. *Womanist Ethics and the Cultural Production of Evil.* New York: Palgrave Macmillan, 2006.
Walker, Alice. *In Search of Our Mother's Gardens: Womanist Prose.* New York: Harcourt Brace Jovanovich, 1983.

On Faith-Based Initiatives

Bartkowski, John, and Helen Regis. *Charitable Choices: Religion, Race, and Poverty.* New York: New York University Press, 2003.
Bositis, David. "Black Churches and the Faith-Based Initiative: Findings from a National Survey." Washington, DC: The Joint Center for Political and Economic Studies, 2006.
Bush, George W. *Rallying the Armies of Compassion.* Washington, DC: The White House, January 2001.
Ehrenreich, Barbara. "The Faith Factor." *The Nation,* 11 November 2004.
Wuthnow, Robert. *Saving America? Faith-Based Services and the Future of Civil Society.* Princeton, NJ: Princeton University Press, 2004.

Index